SpringerBriefs in Education

More information about this series at http://www.springer.com/series/8914

Héfer Bembenutty · Marie C. White
Miriam R. Vélez

Developing Self-regulation of Learning and Teaching Skills Among Teacher Candidates

 Springer

KH

Héfer Bembenutty
Secondary Education and Youth Service
Queens College of The City University
   of New York
Queens, NY
USA

Miriam R. Vélez
School of Education New York City
Nyack College
New York, NY
USA

Marie C. White
School of Education New York City
Nyack College
New York, NY
USA

ISSN 2211-1921   ISSN 2211-193X   (electronic)
SpringerBriefs in Education
ISBN 978-94-017-9949-2   ISBN 978-94-017-9950-8   (eBook)
DOI 10.1007/978-94-017-9950-8

Library of Congress Control Number: 2015940990

Springer Dordrecht Heidelberg New York London

Printed on acid-free paper

Springer Science+Business Media B.V. Dordrecht is part of Springer Science+Business Media
(www.springer.com)

5/9/16

Foreword I

What I found fascinating about this book is its foundation in the social cognitive and self-regulation theories. The theoretical frameworks guide the case study in a way that one can pictorially frame the description of the four teacher candidates with clear delineation. The book invites the reader to join the journey of four teacher candidates, understand their challenges, and admire their resourcefulness in spite of setbacks.

Bembenutty, White, and Vélez are commended in their description of four major hallmarks of academic success and teaching preparation training. The first hallmark is the importance of self-efficacy for all learners. In my own teaching, I have encountered talented students, who in spite of their abilities, were not successful because they had doubts about their competence. Self-beliefs are necessary; a high level of intelligence is not enough to be a successful teacher—self-efficacy is also needed.

The ability to delay gratification is another hallmark clearly delineated in this book. I applaud the authors by taking a leadership in this area, which is so much needed at this time when our young generation is often seduced by instant gratification and immediate rewards. Some college students are not mastering self-control. Nevertheless, in this book, the reader is introduced to four conscientious learners who unlike some of their contemporaries postponed immediate and attractive alternatives to focus on the reward of becoming leaders in our society.

A third hallmark derived from the book is the importance of help seeking as a behavioral and social self-regulated learning strategy. As an educator, I intentionally motivated my students to seek help when needed but some did not. Protection of their self-esteem, concerns about how others could perceive them, and fear of demonstrating incompetence interfered with seeking help. In my work with teachers, I encouraged them to seek help. We conducted several studies that support the findings of the case study.

The last hallmark of this case study is the strong support these four teacher candidates received from their institution and teacher educators. If more educators provide caring and culturally sensitive environments, we could prepare more teachers who are drawn to teach where only a few highly qualified teachers want to teach. Teachers with the drive and motivation of these four teacher candidates could make significant contributions to our urban communities where language barriers, low socioeconomic status, and culturally diverse children often make them feel left out of the mainstream—with these teachers who reflect the passion, caring, and commitment of their institutional core values, those children could build the self-efficacy needed to learn and reach their highest potentials.

Bembenutty, White, and Vélez have provided compelling evidence that self-regulation matters when those who are in question are teacher candidates. I am grateful to the researchers for how this book will add an important area of study to the field of education and psychology. This book is for both teacher educators and teacher candidates to read. If teacher candidates are motivated to be successful, this book tells them how it can be done. If teacher educators want their students to be successful in their programs, this book provides a model of how to transform caterpillars into butterflies and simple birds into giant eagles.

Wilbert (Bill) J. McKeachie
Emeritus Professor
University of Michigan

Foreword II

Drawing on a rich body of research and theory on self-regulation of learning, Bembenutty, White, and Vélez present compelling case studies indicating that the capability of teacher candidates to self-regulate their attainment of educational goals depends on their exposure to self-regulated teacher educators, especially as they model, scaffold, and mentor in classroom settings. This important text gives numerous examples of how teacher educators can become role models and agents for self-regulatory change, and it will be an invaluable resource for courses in education, psychology, and human development.

Barry J. Zimmerman, Professor Emeritus
Graduate Center
The City University of New York

In an effective blend of theory and case histories, Bembenutty, White, and Vélez provide valuable information and advice for prospective teachers and teacher educators. Their focus on help seeking is critical given the array of resources available to overcome early difficulties especially for teachers with significant challenges. Also important is helping them understand the role of delay of gratification in the face of expanding sources of distraction.

Stuart A. Karabenick, Research Professor
University of Michigan

This book builds a really strong case for the importance of self-regulation in teacher education. Moreover, it tells a fascinating story of educational success against the odds, made possible by personal stamina as well as contextual support. Both teacher students and teacher educators around the world will find this book a wonderful inspiration.

Ivar Bråten, Professor
University of Oslo, Norway

This is a practical book which provides a compelling narrative with page after page on teacher self-regulatory functioning. I recommend this book for teacher preparation programs, and I will definitely share it with many of my students and colleagues.

Anastasia Kitsantas, Professor
George Mason University

Preface

The area of research that investigates self-regulation and instruction in teacher candidates and teachers has been largely neglected, considering its relevance to teacher quality, psychological well-being, and students' academic growth. The purpose of this book is to report findings from an in depth case study that examines the associations between teacher candidate's self-regulatory skills and motivational beliefs during their clinical experiences both in the college classroom and school settings from the perspective of social cognitive theory and self-regulation theory.

Self-regulation of learning is known to be important for students in general, but also for teacher candidates and in-service teachers. Learning how to teach is not enough; teachers need to learn how to learn. Teacher education programs can be important contributors to the presence of self-regulated teachers in the classroom. Teacher candidates often have difficulty engaging in adaptive help seeking when a task becomes too difficult to be completed alone. They also have difficulty delaying gratification when distracted from completing a task by invitations to more attractive activities. Often, they maintain low levels of self-efficacy for learning and teacher self-efficacy beliefs that undermine their capability and competence to perform designated and important teaching preparation tasks.

This case study of four teacher candidates was based on an ongoing interest in the success of a teacher preparation program at a small college in an urban setting. The choice of self-regulated learning as a focus for the study is linked to the core values of the college. The enrollment reflects the population of most inner cities providing an edge in developing a program that is effective for urban schools. The college is nationally recognized for its ethnic, socioeconomic, and cultural diversity among students and faculty. The researchers provide an integral account of the self-regulatory and motivational beliefs in a case study format:

- Provide a direct account of the development of four teacher candidates during their student teaching clinical experience.
- Focus on contemporary educational theories to describe and interpret the experience of the four teacher candidates.

- Learn the educational and psychological experiences that impacted their learning and teaching experiences.
- Provide directions for future research derived from the experience of these four teacher candidates and directions for educational practices.

First, the introduction provides an overview of the institution and how the participants were chosen for this study. The following section, the literature review, focuses on the importance of social cognitive theory and self-regulation theory. The next section describes the settings, participants, and assessments used in the case study followed by the outcome of the observations and analyses of surveys and questionnaires. The discussion addresses what really matters. The major findings and educational implications of the case study provide the basis for future studies.

We wanted a book that would showcase the efforts and accomplishments of students who benefitted from a strategic approach towards their successful completion of a teacher preparation program by integrating self-regulatory strategies into the fiber of their learning experiences. The faculty and students worked together to establish a supportive network within and beyond the college whose members encouraged help-seeking, delaying gratification, monitoring self-efficacy for learning, and teacher self-efficacy.

This book is written for teacher candidates to believe that if they heard a call to teach, they can read in each paragraph that they can do it. Teacher candidates reading this book will find themselves vicariously portrayed in the journey of the four aspiring teachers described in this book. They can empathize with their struggles but will also find assurance that through self-regulation, their own journeys and dreams could have great outcomes. This book is also written for teacher educators in teaching education programs to realize that by transforming their curriculum in light of new findings on self-regulation, they could facilitate the training process of teacher candidates under their supervision and to understand that self-regulation of learning and teaching matters for teacher candidates.

This book differs from other books related to teacher candidates in several important ways:

- This book reports the journey of four teacher candidates over the span of 4 years from their initial student teaching experience until 2 years into their professional work.
- This book focuses on the important role of social cognitive theory and self-regulation theory as two umbrellas known to have substantial research evidence of successes.
- This book emphasizes the role of teacher self-efficacy, academic delay of gratification, and help seeking as pivotal factors known to buffer academic success and achievement.
- This book focuses on four teacher candidates from underrepresented ethnic groups who were not expected to survive their rigorous teaching program but who became self-regulated learners by postponing immediately attractive alternatives, seeking help when needed, and by developing self-efficacy.
- This book is rigorous in its methodology by triangulating its data sources, which include observation, questionnaires, archival sources, and reflections.

Acknowledgments

We celebrate and thank the participant teacher candidates because without their contribution this case study would not be possible. We acknowledge the administration and staff of the college who made it possible for our students to attend this institution because they consistently seek to be academically excellent, globally engaged, intentionally diverse, socially relevant, and personally transforming. We thank our families for their continued support while we worked on this book.

Contents

4 School Observations and Classroom Experience 45
   4.1   Observation of Student Teachers 46
   4.2   Rationale for Placement 46
   4.3   School: Public 47
   4.4   School: Private 48
   4.5   Senior Teaching Seminar Assignment 48
   4.6   Observation of Teacher Candidates 50
       4.6.1   Chris 50
       4.6.2   Angela 51
       4.6.3   Jaime 51
       4.6.4   Maria 52
   4.7   Findings Across All Teacher Candidates 53
   References 53

5 Survey: Motivation and Self-regulation 55
   5.1   Introduction 55
   5.2   Instruments 56
   5.3   Correlation Among Variables 59
   5.4   Mean Differences Among Teacher Candidates 60
   5.5   Putting It Together 61
   References 62

6 Student Teaching Interview 63
   6.1   Interview Questions and Example Answers 64
   6.2   What Have We Found So Far? 68
   6.3   Post-graduation Interview 70
   6.4   Examples of Responses to the Post-graduation Questionnaire 71
   6.5   Putting It Together 76
   References 77

7 Putting It All Together: What Really Matters? 79
   7.1   Major Findings: Motivation 80
   7.2   Major Findings: Cognition 81
   7.3   Major Findings: Resource Management 82
   7.4   Major Findings: Academic Environment 82
   7.5   What Is Significant About This Case Study? 83
       7.5.1   College Environment 83
       7.5.2   Personal Commitment 85
   7.6   Limitations of the Case Study 86
   7.7   Educational Implications 87
   7.8   What Can Be Done? 88
   7.9   Self-regulation and the Teacher Candidate 89
   7.10 If You Want a Better Student, Be a Better Teacher! 89
   7.11 The Role of the Teacher Educator 90
   7.12 The Role of the Teacher Candidate 94

About the Authors

Héfer Bembenutty is an assistant professor in Educational Psychology at Queens College of The City University of New York in the Department of Secondary and Youth Services where he is the department coordinator of the Educational Psychology courses, the Research Symposium, and Educational Psychology Lecture Series. Dr. Bembenutty obtained his doctorate from The City University of New York, Graduate Center in educational psychology. He has maintained an active research agenda in students and teachers' self-regulation of learning, homework self-regulation, self-efficacy beliefs, multicultural education, and academic delay of gratification. He has also published studies on teachers' self-efficacy beliefs and self-regulation and has served as an editor for special issue journals. He co-edited *Applications of Self-regulated Learning across Diverse Disciplines: A Tribute to Barry J. Zimmerman*.

Marie C. White is an associate professor in the School of Education at Nyack College. She serves as department chair of both the Childhood and Adolescent Education Departments in New York City. Dr. White obtained her doctorate from The City University of New York, Graduate Center in educational psychology. She maintains an active research agenda in self-regulation of learning, specifically focusing on teacher candidates in the area of academic help seeking. Her research focuses on the self-regulated learning processes that enhance teacher certification experiences through high stakes testing for diverse teacher candidates. Dr. White has a book in press, *Self-regulation and the Common Core: Applications to ELA Standards*, about applying the principles of self-regulation of learning to the common core standards.

Miriam R. Vélez is the Coordinator of Student Teaching and an assistant professor in the School of Education at Nyack College. Certified by New York State in Bilingual Education, she has 30 years of experience as both an inner city and public school instructor. Presently, she serves as the liaison for the college with the city and state departments of education and the edTPA coordinator. In addition, she teaches Foundations of Education, Health Issues, and Methods courses. She has done extensive community-based consulting in the area of education for both poor urban communities and the home schooling network.

Chapter 1
Introduction: The Case Study

A fundamental goal of education is to equip students with self-regulatory capabilities that enable them to evaluate themselves. Self-directedness not only contributes to success in formal instruction but also promotes lifelong learning. Self-regulation encompasses skills for planning, organizing, and managing instructional activities, enlisting resources, regulating one's motivation, and applying metacognitive skills to enable the adequacy of one's knowledge and strategies.

Bandura (1997, pp. 174–175)

Abstract This chapter introduces the book on self-regulation of learning and teaching by providing evidence from research conducted in an urban institution with core values that are aligned with academic, diverse, and transforming principles, which was the perfect choice for a small group of aspiring teachers. Not fully realizing the obstacles to achieving their dreams to make significant contributions to their communities, four teacher candidates entered the arena of a nurturing and caring teacher education program that welcomed the opportunity to turn their dreams into goals. Well aware of the obstacles, faculty members believed self-regulated aspiring teachers could do well in the program in spite of past academic challenges. A well-documented component of the success of the four students presented in this case study is the emphasis the teacher preparation program places on enhancing their self-regulatory skills along with the development of self-efficacy and sense of agency. The researchers employed the case study method to use real time evidence of the teacher candidate's initial steps, trajectories, processes, academic progress, and professional outcomes to provide a holistic and interesting description of four success stories.

Keyword Self-regulation · Teachers · Motivation · Self-efficacy · Delay of gratification · Core values

September of 2007 brought four young students with the aspirations, desires, and dreams to enter a teacher education program at an urban college in the northeastern part of the United States. Without fully comprehending the implications of their

© The Author(s) 2015
H. Bembenutty et al., *Developing Self-regulation of Learning and Teaching Skills Among Teacher Candidates*, SpringerBriefs in Education,
DOI 10.1007/978-94-017-9950-8_1

actions, these students entered the arena of teacher education certification for which they were underprepared. The urban institution the students attended provides opportunities for students who desire to become teachers to qualify for the program in spite of prior academic challenges in their middle and high schools. These students' challenges included prior low academic performance and being educated in underperforming schools, some in economically disadvantaged neighborhoods.

Similar to some other students qualifying to enter the program, they came from underrepresented cultural groups and had experienced personal challenges, which included growing up without both or one of their parents, ethnic discrimination, language barriers, and academic under preparation. As individuals aspiring to become teachers, they found a college that nurtured, scaffolded, and mentored them to take control of their academic and personal futures as well as their professional ambitions. They also came under the supervision of caring educators who introduced them to the teaching profession and helped them attain their goals by working through the processes of self-regulation of learning. These educators were a part of a social environment that encouraged each individual student to grow academically, dispositionally, and socially to reach their highest potential. The developmental process of self-regulation was not an easy task; basic academic skills needed to be acquired, self-confidence needed to be nurtured, ways to seek help needed to be modeled, willingness to delay gratification needed to be enhanced, and the skills of social and environmental control needed to be sculpted. Nevertheless, in the case of these four, and many other students qualifying to be enrolled in the teacher education program, passion for learning was a strong motivator, and their dreams were shaped into goal-oriented behaviors as they moved through the teacher preparation program.

> The purpose of this book is to share the initial steps, trajectories, processes, academic progress, and professional outcomes of four teacher candidates who were followed during a span of 4 years.

The private institution in which these four teacher candidates were enrolled has core values aligned with high academic and performance standards and provides support for students who aspire to become teachers. Founded on spiritual and humanistic values, the institution has educators who promote student-centered education in a stimulating learning environment that fosters student engagement and critical thinking. The educators focus on development of personal and professional identity and development through cooperative learning, ample opportunities to succeed, transformation of limitations into strengths, and active learning. They endorse the importance of help seeking as an educational skill that promotes self-regulation rather than a sense of inferiority.

A well-documented component in the success of these four students has been the effort placed on enhancing their self-regulatory skills along with the development of beliefs and sense of agency. Their teacher training was heavily based on social cognitive theory in which the environment, the individuals, and contextual factors interact to influence personal agency and academic outcomes. Within the context of social cognitive theory, self-regulation of learning was a key factor in their successes as both teacher candidates and college graduates. Self-regulation, as a multidimensional process, enhances learners' ability to pro-actively generate, monitor, and reflect on their learning process. A self-regulation approach takes into consideration learners' thoughts, beliefs, actions, feelings, and emotions while pursuing academic goals. The objective of self-regulation of learning is to empower learners to be self-directed, proactive, and competent learners who identify goals, select strategies to pursue and monitor those goals, and evaluate whether outcomes are consistent with expectations and standards. As self-regulated learners, students use strategies to overcome obstacles and sustain persistence and delay gratification when alternative choices compete for atten-tion (Bandura and Mischel 1965; Bembenutty 2007). These four students were coached, mentored, scaffolded, and nurtured by self-regulated educators who con-sistently and across time modeled skills such as goal setting, self-monitoring, help seeking, and self-evaluation.

The purpose of this book is to share the initial steps, trajectories, processes, academic progress, and professional outcomes of four teacher candidates who were followed during a span of 4 years. Our systematic approach examines their transition from novices struggling to prepare for professional licensing into self-confident and proactive, self-regulated learners. Specifically, we first describe the construct of self-regulation of learning within the social cognitive theory. We then describe the educational setting where these students were enrolled, followed by the description of the individual students. We also describe our methodol-ogy for data collection which included school observations and classroom expe-riences, interviews and surveys, and testimonies from educators and students' post-graduation enterprises, and our outcomes. We conclude with general lessons learned from this case study that could benefit educators and students who are currently facing the challenges of becoming fully certified teachers.

1.1 A General Perspective of the Case Study

The disparity in achievement experienced by students in high needs urban areas when compared with students who have greater economic resources has become a focus in the field of education (Foote 2005). The definition of urban or inner-city is evolving, and it is becoming increasingly more difficult to make distinctions between urban and suburban based on ethnic, socioeconomic, and cultural diversity of populations living in these areas. However, it is agreed that urban schools and teachers have specific characteristics that present unique challenges to educational achievement (Foote 2005). Public schools located in high poverty areas are often lacking in basic instructional resources including technology, textbooks, and qualified teachers. Urban teachers describe their classrooms as overcrowded and struggle with meeting the increased standards with a decline in materials and resources (Maxson et al. 2000). Overcrowding impacts classroom management and the amount of shared space makes it difficult to create a stable learning environment.

As the minority populations in urban centers continue to grow, so does the need for teachers who are bilingual and sensitive to cultural diversity. The demand for highly qualified teachers reflects a nationwide trend: student enrollments are increasing while the supply of highly qualified teachers is declining. There is an acute need for minority teachers in the inner city schools of America. Urban districts lose nearly one half of their newly hired teachers within the first 5 years (Darling-Hammond 2000). The student population is increasingly diverse (Gerdeman 2001) and the public school teacher hiring pool remains predominantly White non-Hispanic (84 %). Research provides evidence of a significantly higher dropout of students of color who enter the teacher education pipeline than their White counterparts. Often, students of color who enter college with the desire to become teachers do not remain in the program, and many do not graduate from college (Vegas et al. 2001; Cochran-Smith and Zeichner 2010). Often, these students enter college without having mastered the basic academic skills, which are required to pass the first state certification exam (Mitchell et al. 2001).

1.2 Procedure in This Case Study

The design and data collection for this case study followed Yin's (2009) three general tactics reporting case studies:

- *Defining a case study*: After considering multiple ways of representing our research, the case study design was selected. We consistently collected data that supported the design, instrumentation, and expected findings of the work we started out to publish. Publications were selected from the peer reviewed research on social cognitive theory and self-regulated learning theory related to learning and achievement among students in general and teacher candidates in particular. We included scholarly work from specific researchers and educators who have conducted studies on self-regulation among teacher candidates (e.g., Myron Dembo, Nancy Perry, Judy Randi) for the literature review. The method section was drafted with a description of instruments and procedures. Several possible ways to analyze descriptive and quantitative data in the case studies were considered before we proceeded. Given that we are quantitative researchers, we were aware that descriptive data would be an adaptation from our traditional way of reporting findings.
- *Case identities: Real or anonymous*: Deciding whether or not to identify the participants by name was challenging. As Yin (2009) advises, disclosure of the identity of the participants is the most desirable option. However, there are advantages and disadvantages for disclosing the participants' identities; therefore, we opted to

use generic names to identify each participant. One advantage of knowing a participant's full identity is that readers are able to make connections between the case
study and the research linking an identified participant to the data. This makes it
easier to associate and interpret the data and reach their own conclusions about the
study. A second advantage is that full disclosure can facilitate the reading of the
case study. However, Yin maintained that on some occasions anonymity is necessary to protect participants from being associated with specific actions in the case
study. We opted to not identify the participants in the case study and changed their
names to support the flow of the document but not reveal actual names.

- *Reviewing the draft case study—A validating procedure*: Yin recommends that
  the validity of the case study be examined. In order to do this, the manuscript
  was sent to reviewers who were asked to use their expertise to judge its validity. On many levels, factual material presented in the case study has been cor-
  roborated. As Yin (2009) also suggests, we fact checked with the participants
  for specific data regarding state certification exam scores to enhance construct
  validity of the study.

1.3 The Present Study Is an Exemplary Case Study

According to Yin (2009), an exemplary case study has five major characteristics.
Based on these five contentions, the present case study is exemplary.

1. *Is the case study significant?* The significance of the case study lies in the participants, their status as teacher candidates, and the link to the theory of self-
   regulation. Specifically, identifying help seeking, delay of gratification, and
   teacher self-efficacy beliefs among teacher candidates is of interest to the general
   population. There has been significantly less research investigating self-regulation
   among teacher candidates in spite of the emphasis on self-regulation among regular learners. The unique profiles of the teacher candidates highlight the importance
   of the present study and make it very interesting to the general population.
2. *Is the case study complete?* The present case study has validity and contains
   multiple data sources such as self-reports, observations, archaic data, pre and
   post-questionnaires, and after graduation assessments. These assessments are
   comprehensive in the sense that they encompass most major aspects of teacher
   preparation programs.
3. *Did the case study consider alternative perspectives?* We considered rival
   propositions. For instance, we considered different theories, which could provide alternative explanations to the findings. We considered different interpreta-
   tions to the data we obtained.
4. *Did the case study display sufficient evidence?* We provided sufficient evidence
   for our claims. To illustrate, with regard to the concept of teacher self-efficacy, we
   observed the participants and administered pre and post-questionnaires for them
   to engage in self-analysis of their self-efficacy beliefs. We also observed them in

the classroom teaching actual students and in the college classrooms displaying their beliefs among peers. The triangulation of data validated the evidence.

5. *Was the case study composed in an engaging manner?* Our report attempted to engage the readers through real time evidence of actual experiences of teacher candidates.

Table 1.1 Outline of the case study procedures

Task	Procedure
Type of study	Case study of teaching experiences of four teacher candidates during practical and clinical experiences in urban classroom settings
Theoretical framework	Social cognitive theory and self-regulation of learning theory guided the researchers examined as they examined: (1) The association between the self-regulatory skills and motivational beliefs and student teaching experience (2) The association between self-regulatory and motivational tendencies in the context of a teacher preparation program with an emphasis on teacher self-efficacy, help-seeking, and academic delay of gratification
Sample of variables assessed	Self-regulatory strategy use: (1) Academic delay of gratification (2) Help-seeking Self-efficacy: (1) Self-efficacy for learning (2) Teacher self-efficacy Cognitive, motivational, and self-regulatory perception of their learning and teaching preparation from their own perspective and report
Method of assessment	(1) Survey in the form of a questionnaire (completed by teacher candidates during student teaching experience) (2) Structured interviews (3) Observations (real-time)
Major findings	The results indicate that teacher candidates who have positive attitudes towards self-regulation, self-efficacy beliefs, delay of gratification, and positive help seeking tendencies were those who reported high teaching self-efficacy beliefs and engaged frequently in help seeking when it was necessary. In addition, teacher candidates with a positive attitude towards help seeking and self-regulation were those who preferred to delay gratification and evidenced high self-efficacy
Main conclusions	(1) Self-regulation matters for the academic success and teaching preparation training of teacher candidates (2) Self-regulation is associated with academic performance of teacher candidates (3) Academic delay of gratification, self-efficacy, intrinsic motivation, and help-seeking strategies are associated with successful teacher preparation completion (4) Self-regulation, help seeking, academic delay of gratification, and self-efficacy appear to buffet the teaching preparation training of teacher candidates who were initially at risk for completing the program (5) Positive environment, caring educators, supportive peers, and institutional core values and philosophy are elements that foster self-regulation of learning among teacher candidates from a diverse background

In the past, case studies were considered less desirable than experimental or survey studies. However, there is enough evidence that the case study research method is evolving and the one presented in this book meets the standard of what has become a commonly used method in conducting evaluations (Yin 2009).

- *Does the case study have rigor?* The present study followed a systematic procedure and avoided bias.
- *Is there basis for scientific generalization?* The present study could help all education programs around the nation if they want to implement self-regulation in their teaching programs. Our study includes underrepresented teacher candidates who went from developmental courses to master's degree programs and of whom three are now teachers and the fourth has a successful career with law firm teaching non-English speaking immigrants how the justice system works. These students are representative of many enrolled in most institutions of higher education.
- *Did the case study take an extended amount of time to be completed?* Yes, our study actually has taken 4 years to be completed. The longitudinal study followed the participants over an extended period of time beyond the initial observations to insure validity.
- *Is the case study randomized?* The presented case study does not claim cause and effect. It is not a true experiment in which effects are experimentally manipulated with particular treatment and control groups.

Table 1.1 displays the outline of the study. The outline describe the type of study, its theoretical framework, sample of variables assessed, methods of assessment, major findings, and main conclusions (Goetz et al. 2013).

References

Bandura, A. (1997). *Self-efficacy: The exercise of control.* New York, NY: W. H. Freeman.

Bandura, A., & Mischel, W. (1965). Modifications of self-imposed delay of reward through exposure to live and symbolic models. *Journal of Personality and Social Psychology, 2,* 698–705. doi:10.1037/h0022655.

Bembenutty, H. (2007). Self-regulation of learning and academic delay of gratification: Gender and ethnic differences among college students. *Journal of Advanced Academics, 18*(4), 586–616.

Cochran-Smith, M., & Zeichner, K. M. (Eds.). (2010). *Studying teacher education: The report of the AERA panel on research and teacher education.* New York, NY: Routledge.

Darling-Hammond, L. (2000). *Solving the dilemmas of teacher, supply, demand, and quality.* New York, NY: National Commission on Teaching and America's Future.

Foote, C. J. (2005). The challenge and potential of high-need urban education. *The Journal of Negro Education, 74*(4), 371–381.

Gerdeman, R. D. (2001). ERIC review: The role of community colleges in training tomorrow's school teachers. *Community College Review, 28*(4), 62–76.

Goetz, T., Nett, U. E., & Hall, N. C. (2013). Self-regulated learning. In N. C. Hall & T. Goetz (Eds.), *Emotion, motivation, and self-regulation: A handbook for teachers.* Emerald: Bingley, UK.

Maxson, S., Wright, C. R., Houck, J. W., Lynn, P., & Fowler, L. (2000). Urban teachers' views on areas of need for K-12/university collaboration. *Action in Teacher Education, 22*(2), 39–53.

Mitchell, K. J., Robinson, D. Z., Plake, B. S., & Knowles, K. T. (Eds.). (2001). *Testing teacher candidates: The role of licensure tests in improving teacher quality.* Washington, DC: National Academy Press.

Vegas, E., Murnana, R. I., & Willett, J. B. (2001). From high school to teaching: Many steps, who makes it? *Teachers College Record, 103*(3), 427–449.

Yin, R. K. (2009). *Case study research: Design and methods* (4th ed.). Thousand Oaks, CA: Sage.

Chapter 2
Self-regulated Learning and Development in Teacher Preparation Training

> *Students are self-regulated to the degree that they are metacognitively, motivationally, and behaviorally active participants in their own learning process. These students self-generate thoughts, feelings, and actions to attain their learning goals.*
>
> Zimmerman (2001, p. 5).

Abstract Social cognitive theory emphasizes the importance of human agency and provides a framework to study how learners acquire competencies, skills, dispositions, beliefs, and self-regulation. This chapter argues that self-regulated learning and development is one way in which social cognitive theory has been applied to preparing future teachers. In addition, self-efficacy, individuals' belief about their capability to perform a specific task, has been associated with academic achievement among teacher candidates. Specifically, the cyclical phases of self-regulation described here provide a framework to train teacher candidates to become proactive and goal directed learners and practitioners. Learning to teach is not enough for today's teacher candidates, therefore, integration of crucial self-regulatory learning strategies into their curricula is recommended by researchers to put future teachers in charge of their learning processes. In general, this chapter reviews the existing literature on self-regulation of learning and motivation, and among teacher candidates who struggle with personal and academic challenges specifically.

Keywords Self-regulation · Teacher candidates · Motivation · Social cognitive theory · Self-regulation theory · Self-efficacy · Learning skills

Since Bandura's (1977) introduction of social cognitive theory explaining how learners acquire competencies, skills, dispositions, beliefs, and self-regulation, educators and researchers have increasingly applied his theory to different aspects of learning and development (Bembenutty et al. 2013; Boekaerts et al. 2000; Corno 1993; Winne 1997; Zimmerman and Schunk 2011). *Self-regulation*

H. Bembenutty et al., *Developing Self-regulation of Learning and Teaching Skills Among Teacher Candidates*, SpringerBriefs in Education,
DOI 10.1007/978-94-017-9950-8_2

of learning refers to students' self-generated thoughts, feelings, and actions that are systematically designed to affect learning of knowledge and skills (Zimmerman 2000). Zimmerman construes self-regulated learners as individuals who are cognitively, motivationally, and behaviorally active participants in their own learning process. During the last few decades, self-regulation of learning has acquired a pivotal role in all areas of learning including sport and academic learning; medical and music fields; and mathematics, sciences, and technological disciplines (Acevedo et al. 2007; Bembenutty et al. 2013). There is a global interest in self-regulation theory with the most notable research and interventions in self-regulation being conducted in Africa, South and North America, Europe, Australia, and Asian countries (Bembenutty et al. 2013; Vohs and Baumeister 2011).

Four models of self-regulated learning emerge from amongst those that have been most commonly employed in educational research and instruction. Winne, Boekaerts, Pintrich, and Zimmerman share the investigation of five underlying issues: (1) What motivates students to self-regulate during learning? (2) What processes or procedures engages students in becoming self-aware of self-reactive? (3) What are the key processes and responses that self-regulated students use to reach academic goals? (4) How is student's self-regulated learning affected by the social and physical environment? (5) How is the capacity to self-regulate when learning acquired by the learner? (Zimmerman and Schunk 2011). The case study focuses on Zimmerman's model because it has been applied extensively in developmental research emphasizing the importance of social relationships in learning.

Winne's inclusion of the recursive feedback loop in his information processing model of self-regulated learning (Winne and Perry 2000) provides learners with distinctive forms of cues, feedback, and supplementary information as they learn new instructional material in accordance with their phase of self-regulated learning (Zimmerman and Schunk 2011). This model focuses on the learner's metacognition, defined as awareness of one's own strength and abilities in relation to the task demands, and specific ways in which learners cognitively adapt to the task demands to regulate their learning strategies.

Boekaerts' model of self-regulated learning looks at learning episodes, in which learners are asked to demonstrate context-specific, goal-directed learning behavior (Boekaerts and Niemivirta 2000). An important point of this model is that learners are encouraged to co-create learning episodes that will help them to reach their own goals—as opposed to participating in episodes created exclusively by the teacher. Self-regulation involves being able to adapt to various learning episodes, including those set by the teacher.

Pintrich's model suggests that self-regulated learning occurs in four phases with processes falling into cognitive, motivational/affective, behavioral, and contextual areas (Pintrich 2000). The first phase is forethought, planning, and activation. The second phase is the monitoring phase during which learners are engaging in metacognitive awareness and monitoring of various processes (e.g., cognition, motivation, and affect), of the effort and time needed to complete the task, and of the changing task and contextual conditions. In the third phase of control, learners select and adapt cognitive strategies for learning and thinking. They manage motivation and affect, increase or decrease effort, seek help, change or negotiate the task, and change or leave the learning context. In the final phase, learners are believed to react and reflect by forming cognitive judgments and attributions, choosing behavior, and evaluating the task and learning context.

Research on self-regulation has revealed that in practically all levels of learning enterprises, when learners engage in self-regulatory processes such as goal-setting, self-monitoring, self-evaluation, and self-reflection, students achieve high levels of personal, academic, and professional outcomes in diverse contexts and social domains. For instance, in the medical field, studies have found the ability of the patient to control the illness through an effective therapeutic plan is significantly influenced by social and behavioral factors (Clark 2013; Clark and Zimmerman 2014). Similarly, physical education students who are successful learners engage in self-observation, emulation and self-control, self-regulating their behavior, and controlling their actions during practice sessions. Over the last 40 years, scholars have introduced numerous theories of self-regulation (Boekaerts 1997; Pintrich 1999; Winne 1996, 2001; Zimmerman 2000).

Based on Bandura's social cognitive theory, Zimmerman's (2000) comprehensive theory of self-regulation has generated numerous applications to sports, music, medicine, and learning disciplines, and has been tested and replicated over time. Foundational to any discussion of Zimmerman's theory is a thorough introduction of Bandura's social cognitive theory. The following section includes an overview of social cognitive theory and self-efficacy beliefs, specifically teacher-self efficacy.

2.1 Bandura's Social Cognitive Theory

Bandura introduced social cognitive theory as a reaction to previous theories that emphasized that individuals are subjected to environmental influences, which reduces their behaviors to stimulus control through reinforcement and punishment. Bandura emphasized that individuals learn within a social context through interactions with their environment and by observational learning. He proposed a triadic approach of reciprocity in which the individuals influence the environment and the environment influences the individuals and the behaviors. In turn, behaviors influence both the individuals and the environments. Triadic reciprocality (see Fig. 2.1) represents human functioning as involving complex reciprocal interactions under the control of the individual.

> Social cognitive theory considers individuals to be agents of change who develop and adapt with the intention to influence their own functioning and goals while maintaining control over their outcomes and environment.

Fig. 2.1 Triadic reciprocality
in social cognitive theory

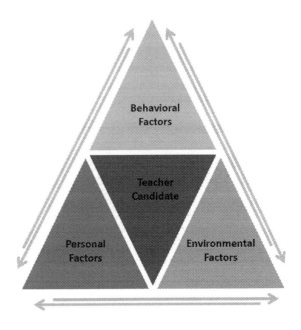

Social cognitive theory considers individuals to be agents of change who develop and adapt with the intention to influence their own functioning and goals while maintaining control over their outcomes and environment. Bandura construes individuals as able to engage in self-organization, proactive learning, self-regulation, and self-reflection (Bandura 1997). Social cognitive theory is founded upon four core properties of human agency: intentionality, forethought, self-reactiveness, and self-reflectiveness (see Table 2.1).

- *Intentionality* involves proactivity and specific planning measures for how one will pursue goals. For example, how willing is a college student to set aside 2 h to complete a homework assignment rather than going out to a party with his friends?
- *Forethought* involves goal setting while considering outcomes. An example of the forethought core property is when a student independently turns off his cellphone in order to avoid a distracting call since he knows that chatting with his friend will preclude him from completing the homework within the time frame of his homework schedule.
- *Self-reactiveness involves* self-monitoring one's goals and maintaining control over the plans to attain those goals. In the case of the homework, the student periodically evaluates the quality of the homework while he is working on the task in light of the standards and rubrics provided by the instructor.
- *Self-reflectiveness* involves self-examination of outcomes, thoughts, actions, feelings, behavior, and personal efficacy. For instance, a student would be careful to pay close attention to his evaluations and reactions to the complete

Table 2.1   Social cognitive theory's core properties of human agency

Core of human agency	Description	Role of teacher educators	Role of teacher candidates
Intentionality	Forming intentions that include actions, plans, and strategies for realizing them	Instruct and model how intentions influence the outcome of specific assignments	Include the use of study logs to state intended outcomes and track how those outcomes are realized
Forethought	Setting goals and anticipating likely outcomes of prospective actions to guide and motivate efforts	Emphasize the significant role of goal setting and goal properties and their influence in setting up a sequence of actions that lead to successful task completion	Set goals by including properties that sequence the actions that will lead to successful task completion
Self-reactiveness	Adopting personal standards, monitoring, and regulating actions by self-reactive influence and by doing tasks that result in self-satisfaction and self-worth	Give students examples of tasks with self-administered consequences that can enhance motivation	Set standards for proximal sub-goals and monitor them while increasing self-efficacy beliefs
Self-reflectiveness	Self-reflecting on the level of self-efficacy, thoughts, and actions, and by making adjustments if necessary	Model adjustments to own teaching and strategies to increase students' familiarity with how easily adjustments can be made when necessary	Examine the degree of self-satisfaction with the completed task and incorporate feedback when planning improvements for how a similar task can be completed with some adjustments

homework task. Based on the outcomes, the student considers his options to improve his performance. He can invite input from a knowledgeable peer or his teacher for feedback about the quality of the homework rather than solely rely on his self-reflections.

Consistent with Bandura's four core properties of human agency, skilled learners are those who independently activate cognition, affect, and behavior in order to pursue goals and reflect on outcomes. They are agents of social change who influence their environments rather than become subject to environmental influences, reinforcement, and punishment. In addition, they exercise control of situations that impact their learning experiences with their competencies, self-beliefs, and outcome expectancies. Their self-beliefs help them in becoming proactive human agents who act intentionally and are academically successful. These four core properties are intentionally designed to influence students' increased self-beliefs in their skills and competencies to complete challenging tasks, their self-efficacy.

Of all the components of social cognitive theory, one of Bandura's greatest contributions was the importance of self-efficacy beliefs for academic success as the cornerstone of all human agencies (Bandura 1977).

2.2 Self-efficacy for Learning

Self-efficacy refers to individuals' beliefs about their capability to perform designated tasks (Bandura 1997; Usher and Pajares 2008). According to Bandura, individuals' self-perceptions of capability are instrumental to successful goal attainment and to the control of the process and outcomes of reaching those goals. Exercising environmental control and managing social interactions depend on the level of self-belief in one's capabilities. For instance, a learner who does not believe that he can master an important homework task would have difficulty completing the task successfully because levels of self-efficacy influence the degree of effort one will give for a specific task. A learner with low self-efficacy would easily become distracted and readily divert his attention from completing the task. A learner with high self-efficacy will delay gratification, remaining focused on the task to complete the assignment successfully.

Bandura believed a high degree of self-efficacy is necessary to engage in self-control of behaviors, actions, and thoughts or self-regulated learning. Proactive and self-regulated leaners have high levels of self-efficacy that help them to sustain motivation when tasks become difficult. However, learners' who have low levels of self-efficacy beliefs would not be capable of putting sufficient effort into highly demanding tasks. Self-efficacy influences choice, effort, perseverance, resiliency, stress and anxiety. In order to be a self-regulated learner, an appropriate level of self-efficacy is required.

Further investigation into self-efficacy delineates three dimensions: magnitude, strength, and generality (Pajares 1996). *Magnitude* involves the level of task difficulty. For instance, a student who judges a trigonometry homework assignment as highly challenging has assessed the magnitude of the assignments difficulty. *Strength* involves the degree of self-efficacy for a designated task. For example, a student may vary in degrees of self-efficacy for specific tasks. He might have a higher degree of self-efficacy for algebra homework than for trigonometry based on his past experiences with each subject. *Generality* involves the degree to which the capability to engage a task can be extended into a different content or a different situation. To illustrate, if a student's self-beliefs are not generalized to mathematics, he may believe that he can complete the algebra task successfully but not the trigonometry assignment (see Table 2.2).

The association between self-efficacy and academic achievement is supported by research investigating self-efficacy of learning among college students. Under the umbrella of the social cognitive theory of self-regulation of learning, Bembenutty and White (2013) examined the association between homework practices of college students, self-efficacy, self-regulation of learning, and final

Table 2.2 Dimensions of self-efficacy

Dimensions	Descriptions	Examples
Magnitude	Difficulty level (e.g. easy, moderate, difficult) that an individual believes is required to perform a certain task	Teacher candidates have different levels of self-efficacy to write and carry out a lesson plan for a specific setting. The lowest level of confidence can lead to poor performance. When teacher candidates assesses the level of difficulty and ask for help from their cooperating teacher or advisor, their self-efficacy for delivering the lesson increases and their performance is evidence of their beliefs in their abilities to carry out their plan successfully
Strength	Amount of conviction an individual has about performing successfully at diverse levels of difficulty, level of confidence to excel at specific tasks	Teacher candidates ask themselves how confident they are that they will be able to carry out the lesson plan in a diverse setting so that all students have the opportunity to learn. Rating one's level of confidence before and after delivering a lesson plan can increase self-efficacy in teacher candidates' confidence when the learning outcomes are successful. If the teachers' self-efficacy decreases, attribution can be made to specific moments when the teacher candidate became unsure of the planned lesson or ability to carry out the plan effectively
Generality	Degree to which the expectation of successful task completion is generalized across situations, students can perceive themselves as self-efficacious in a range of activities or within one domain of functioning	Most teacher candidates choose to teach lessons in areas where self-efficacy is high, and are less likely to choose areas in which they have lower self-efficacy. Knowing strengths and weaknesses when assessing areas of concentration or expertise is important to future teaching and learning experiences. Attributing a weak delivery of a lesson plan in mathematics to one's lack of content knowledge can encourage the teacher candidates to take additional math classes or work with a tutor

course grades. The results indicated that students with high self-efficacy beliefs were those who also reported intrinsic motivation and engaging in help seeking. Recordings in their individual homework logs suggested that the relationship between students' beliefs and homework practices were associated with their academic performance, adaptive help seeking, and self-efficacy beliefs. More specifically, White and Bembenutty (2013) examined teacher candidate's use of help-seeking strategies and self-efficacy beliefs for preparing to pass a state certification examination. They found that self-efficacy was positively related to teacher candidates' help-seeking strategies, adaptive self-regulatory strategies, and willingness to delay gratification. Educators and aspiring educators also need to have teachers' self-efficacy.

2.3 Teacher's Self-efficacy Beliefs

Enhancing teachers' self-efficacy beliefs of teacher candidates is critical to their performance as teachers and student learning. *Teachers' self-efficacy* refers to teachers' "beliefs in their ability to have a positive effect on student learning" (Ashton 1985, p. 142). According to Tschannen-Moran and Hoy (2001) teachers' self-efficacy beliefs influence teachers' attitudes towards helping their students, their level of satisfaction, and their desire to motivate their students. Teachers' efficacy beliefs guide teacher candidate's professional development during their teacher education preparation programs and after completion of their initial teaching certification (Tschannen-Moran and Hoy 2001).

Bembenutty (2006) investigated the link between teachers' self-efficacy beliefs and academic performance and found support for the association between self-efficacy beliefs and use of self-regulatory learning strategies. Furthermore, Bembenutty and Chen (2005), examined teachers effectiveness and self-efficacy and found additional support for these associations between teachers' beliefs and self-regulatory skills. In a consistent vein, White and Bembenutty (2013) found that self-efficacy is essential to teachers' successful academic performance. Their results revealed that students' tendencies for help seeking vary according to their teachers' self-efficacy beliefs and use of self-regulatory strategies such as delay of gratification.

2.4 Self-regulation of Learning

Bandura (1977) introduced the concept of self-regulation as part of human agency and exercise of control. To Bandura, self-regulation encompassed an essential component of humanness with self-control of individuals over their situations, environments, and contexts. Individuals are not subjected to stimulus control; rather they exercise cognitive, emotional, and behavioral power over their surroundings. Human thought, affect, and behavior are influenced by the ways in which events are construed and depend upon beliefs. Bandura posited that individuals are not just reactors to external stimuli, but that they exercise influence over their environment and own behavior (Bandura 1977). Zimmerman (2000) has successfully applied the concept of self-regulation to academic contexts.

According to Zimmerman (2000), self-regulation of learning is a fundamental element for all academic enterprise and success. Self-regulated learners engage in actions, thoughts, and behaviors in order to pursue determined tasks. They do so by identifying goals and strategies and by monitoring and evaluating them. Over the past decades, scholars and educators have consistently demonstrated the efficacy of self-regulation on enhancing learning and sustaining goals over significant periods. Self-regulation involves motivation, cognition, and resource management (Pintrich and De Groot 1990; Pintrich et al. 1993).

2.5   Cyclical Phases of Self-regulation

Zimmerman conceptualized self-regulation as a cyclical process with three phases: forethought, performance, and self-reflection. The phases are cyclical because each process within each phase of self-regulation influences the next one. For instance, after students have engaged in self-reflection, they continue the cycle in forethought with a new task or a revision of the previous one. Given the level of performance, the students adjust and adapt their actions, behavior, and beliefs while tackling a new, similar, task. As Kitsantas and Dabbagh (2010) observed, "The cycle of learning promotes individual empowerment, in part because it reinforces the beliefs of the individual in his or her ability to effectively control aspects of the learning experience toward a desired outcome" (p. 11). In a similar vein, Zimmerman (2000) describes the structure of self-regulatory systems in these terms:

> From a social cognitive perspective, self-regulatory processes and accompanying beliefs fall into three cyclical phases: forethought, performance or volitional control, and self-reflection phases. Forethought refers to influential processes that precede efforts to act and set the stage for it. Performance or volitional control involves processes that occur during motoric efforts and affect attention and action. Self-reflection involves processes that occur after performance efforts and influence a person's response to that experience. These self-reflections, in turn, influence forethought regarding subsequent motoric efforts—thus completing a self-regulatory cycle. (p. 16)

The three phases of self-regulation are (see Fig. 2.2):

- The *forethought phase:* learners are proactive agents who set short and long-term goals, identify strategies to pursue those goals, and assess their self-efficacy beliefs and intrinsic interest on those tasks as well as their goal orientation.
- The *performance phase*: learners engage in self-monitoring and self-control of those goals, strategies, and motivation while seeking help from knowledgeable individuals and delay gratification when it is necessary for the sake of completing goals.
- The *self-reflection phase*: learners engage in self-evaluation of tasks completed, examine their level of self-satisfaction and adapt to their circumstances by determining whether tasks need to be repeated and whether the cycle will move on to a new task if the previous one is considered at a satisfactory level (see Table 2.3).

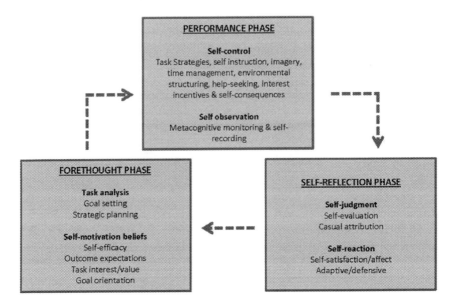

Fig. 2.2 Phases of self-regulated learning

Table 2.3 displays the applications of the cyclical phases of self-regulation, its subprocesses and descriptions, and examples highlighting teacher educators' responsibilities and teacher candidates' tasks. To illustrate, during the forethought phase, a highlighted subprocess is goal setting. The responsibility of teacher educators is to demonstrate goal setting as a critical segment of teaching and learning while the teacher candidates set goals that are suitable to the tasks. In this phase, strategic planning is another subprocess of self-regulation. The responsibility of teacher educators is to require early action planning to be task-specific and reflected in a daily planner while the teacher candidates record action plans in a weekly planner to set up tasks strategically by giving adequate time to carry out the plan.

During the performance phase, self-monitoring is a highlighted subprocess. During this subprocess, teacher educators remind teacher candidates to evaluate their self-efficacy by examining their strengths and weaknesses for a specific task performance. Concurrently, teacher candidates monitor their self-efficacy for doing the tasks by tracing the effectiveness of the chosen strategy. In this phase, help seeking is another subprocess of self-regulation. The responsibility of teacher educators is to remove the negative stigma from asking for help by identifying and defining strategic help seeking behaviors while the teacher candidates proactively seek help from appropriate resources.

During the self-reflection phase, self-evaluation is a subprocess in which the teacher educators provide clear criteria for teacher candidates to compare their work to the standard while teacher candidates use criteria and goal-related

Table 2.3 Cyclical phases of self-regulation and applications to teacher candidates

Cyclical phases of self-regulation	Subprocesses of self-regulation	Description of the sub-processes of self-regulation	Teacher educator's responsibilities to enhance acquisition of the self-regulatory skills	Teacher candidate's tasks to acquire self-regulatory skills
Forethought	Goal Setting	Setting specific high quality proximal goals	Demonstrate goal setting as a critical segment of teaching and learning	Set proximal goals that are suitable to the task
	Strategic Planning	Choosing a specific strategy to meet the demands of the task	Require early planning to be task specific and reflected in a daily planner	Record plan in daily planner to set up tasks strategically giving adequate time to carry out the plan
	Self-efficacy	Individual beliefs in one's capability to learn a specific task	Provide opportunities for goal attainment that lead to increased motivation and higher levels of self-efficacy	Set goals for specific tasks that enhance self-efficacy
	Goal Orientation	Learning or mastery of goal orientation	Provide challenging tasks that enhance students' abilities	Set up self-reminders of course goals for times when a low grade might discourage motivation
	Outcome Expectancy	Anticipated consequences of actions	Link outcome expectancy to goals by modeling self-set goals and personal outcome expectations	When setting a goal link a predicted outcome expectation for that goal
	Intrinsic Interest	Interest in task generated from self-motivation while working on task	Encourage thinking and discussion on how different classes are approached to ascertain interests and motivation	Begin goals with "I enjoy to" to encourage interest in the task
Performance	Attention Focusing	Remain focused on performance, not easily distracted	Demonstrate strategies for capturing attention when bored	Make check marks on a notepad when daydreaming to focus attention on tasks
	Self-instruction	Uses imagery and self-verbalizations to control performance	Model self-instruction by using self-talk to work through problem solving	Use specific self-talk phrases to move through a learning task

(continued)

Table 2.3 (continued)

Cyclical phases of self-regulation	Subprocesses of self-regulation	Description of the sub-processes of self-regulation	Teacher educator's responsibilities to enhance acquisition of the self-regulatory skills	Teacher candidate's tasks to acquire self-regulatory skills
	Self-monitoring	Knowing when one is performing well and when one is not	Remind students to keep track of their self-efficacy to manage their strengths and weaknesses for a specific task performance	Monitor self-efficacy for doing the task tracing the effectiveness of chosen strategy
	Delay of Gratification	Postponing a pleasurable activity (party) until after homework or studying for a test	Frequently remind students how to manage distractions that come from social sources and not allow them to interfere with completing a task	Set priorities that list task completion before social activities and rewards for completing a task on time
	Time Management	Planning tasks using time frames and by predicting and monitoring time allotment	Use time management tools in teaching and learning segments helping students to raise awareness of how much time it takes to complete a specific task	Manage time by prioritizing tasks and systematically scheduling time for each task to be completed in a specific time frame
	Self-consequences	Setting up rewards for completing work on time	Arrange assigned tasks to include a reward system for when work is completed within the set time frame	Use self-rewards to increase motivation when a challenging task becomes too difficult to complete
	Environmental Control	Managing distractions by turning off cell phone or computer access	Give students choices regarding *where* they work and *with whom* they work best	Assess environmental conditions when working on a task and make the decision to change *where* the task can best be completed successfully
	Help Seeking	Asking for a hint or response from a peer or teacher to move forward with a task	Remove the negative stigma from asking for help by identifying and defining strategic help seeking behaviors	Be proactive and seek help from appropriate resources

(continued)

Table 2.3   (continued)

Cyclical phases of self-regulation	Subprocesses of self-regulation	Description of the sub-processes of self-regulation	Teacher educator's responsibilities to enhance acquisition of the self-regulatory skills	Teacher candi-date's tasks to acquire self-regulatory skills
Self-reflection	Self-evaluation	Seek out opportunities to reflect and evaluate performance	Provide clear criteria for students to compare their work to the standard	Use criteria and goal related com-parisons to evalu-ate performance
	Attributions	Find a connec-tion between performance to strategy use rather than low ability	Focus students on their efforts rather than task conditions when providing feedback for work that has been com-pleted successfully or unsuccessfully	Look for strengths and weaknesses to attribute successful and unsuccessful task completion
	Self-reactions	Look for the more effective methods of completing the task than those used	Provide models of completed tasks delin-eating the strategies that led to successful task completion	Remain open to attempting new methods of doing specific types of tasks even though others might be more familiar and less challenging
	Self-satisfaction	Evaluate how well the task was completed and if the standard was met	Establish optimum learning by establish-ing goals and actions plans with students that provide criteria for checking how well their work met the standard	Use feedback from the teacher to assess how well one's own work compares with the standard for the task
	Adaptivity	Use feedback from the self-reflection phase to strengthen or preserve fore-thought beliefs	Assist students when using feedback and self-evaluations to make decisions about how to plan and complete similar assignments in the future successfully	Incorporate feedback and self-evaluations when beginning a task similar to the one completed

comparisons to evaluate performance. In this phase, self-satisfaction is another subprocess of self-regulation in which the responsibility of teacher educators is to provide criteria for checking how well students' work met the standard while the teacher candidates use feedback from the teacher to assess how well one's own work compares with the standard for the task.

Table 2.4 Developmental levels of self-regulation

Developmental levels of self-regulation	Role of the teacher educator	Role of the teacher candidate
Observation	Demonstrate self-evaluation strategies used to identify strengths and weaknesses	Attend to how the model uses self-evaluation strategies to identify strength and weaknesses
Emulation	Encourage students to discuss critical components of self-evaluation	Describe and demonstrate the use of self-evaluation strategies
Self-control	Provide assistance and feedback while monitoring student's use of self-evaluation strategies	Practice using self-evaluation strategies
Self-regulation	Encourage use of self-evaluation for tasks assigned to be completed independently	Consistently use self-evaluation strategies to assist independent self-evaluation

2.6 Why Is the Cyclical Process of Self-regulation Important for Teacher Candidates?

Teacher candidates need to learn how to be self-regulated. As Dembo (2001) has observed, learning to teach is not enough; teachers need to learn how to learn. Similarly, Randi (2004) argued that teacher preparation programs should consider integrating acquisition of crucial self-regulatory learning strategies into their curricula. During childhood and adolescence, students are guided by parents and teachers, but in post-secondary education, learners need to be self-directed, proactive, and in charge of their learning process. This approach is more salient for teacher candidates who need to foster self-assessment, self-reflection, and self-directed learning among their future students.

2.7 Research Evidence of the Applications of the Cyclical Phases of Self-regulation to Teacher Candidates

White and Bembenutty (2013) conducted a study to examine teacher candidates' help- seeking tendencies while preparing to take a teacher certification exam, the LAST (Liberal Arts and Sciences Test). Two complementary theoretical models guided the study: achievement goal theory and self-regulation theory. Specifically, they assessed the different help-seeking orientations of teacher candidates, in particular, teacher candidates' use of avoidance, adaptive, and non-adaptive help-seeking strategies in order to master the content of a state certification exam. Participants in the study were teacher candidates drawn from a small private urban college.

The results revealed that students' tendencies for help seeking vary according to their goal tendencies, teacher self-efficacy beliefs, and use of self-regulatory strategies, such as delay of gratification. These findings suggest that teacher candidates used help seeking as a self-regulatory learning strategy while pursuing academic goals. They also found correlations between LAST scores, teacher self-efficacy beliefs, self-efficacy for learning, and delay of gratification, self-regulation, intrinsic motivation, and help seeking. White and Bembenutty argued that the results of their study were consistent with the self-regulatory approach of help seeking. They also reported that in their study, self-efficacy had a direct association with academic performance and help seeking.

White (2011) examined the help-seeking behaviors of teacher candidates who are at risk for failure of state certification examinations through use of a scale adapted to the arena of teacher education, the Preservice Teacher Help Seeking Scales (PTHSS). In the past, self-report measures of help-seeking behavior patterns have been problematic due to scales with limited reliability, which were not designed to be used in teacher education.

The study was conducted under the umbrella of help seeking as a self-regulatory strategy. White (2011) argued that specifically for aspiring teachers help seeking has not always been construed as a proactive, social behavior helpful to learning and that rather, help seeking has often been viewed as a sign of dependence, and as a result, many learners avoid seeking help. Consistent with Nelson-Le Gall (1981), White distinguished instrumental help seeking and executive help seeking. Instrumental help seeking is when learners seek help in order to master and learn tasks (also labeled adaptive help seeking) and executive help seeking happens when learners seek help for someone to do the task for them (also labeled non-adaptive help seeking). Participants in the study were 50 teacher candidates enrolled in a private college. Help seeking was assessed by:

- *Instrumental help seeking* measured instrumental (adaptive) help seeking from an instructor (5-items, a Likert scale).
- *Executive help seeking* measured executive (non-strategic help seeking) help seeking from an instructor (5-items, a Likert scale).
- *Help seeking avoidance* measured help avoidance (9-items, a Likert scale)
- *Help seeking benefits* assessed teacher candidates' perception about how beneficial help seeking is for them (7-items, a Likert scale).

The results revealed that teacher candidates who reported strategic help-seeking skills were more likely to learn how to pass the certification exams than teacher candidates with nonstrategic help seeking skills. White concluded that training teacher candidates on how to seek help enhances their use of help seeking as a self-regulatory strategy which in turn will result in passing state certification exams.

2.8   Developmental Levels of Self-regulation

Self-regulation is a social enterprise that involves a learner and a knowledgeable individual who can guide the learner through the process of acquiring self-regulatory skills. Consistent with Bandura (1997), modeling involves four processes: attention, retention, practice, and motivation/reinforcement. According to Zimmerman, learners start the self-regulatory process by observing a skilled model. In the case of teacher candidates, the development of self-regulation requires an active learner sensitive to the social cues:

- Attention: Modeling will not occur unless observers are attentive to relevant environmental events.
- Retention: Observers use their cognitive skills and resources to process and retain observed patterns in their short and long-term memory.
- Production: Observers translate their mental conceptions of modeled events into actual behaviors, such as when they translate their thoughts into written sentences and paragraphs.
- Motivation: Observational learning requires certain influences because when students believe that models possess a useful skill they are likely to attend to such models and attempt to retain what they learn (Schunk and Zimmerman 2007).

Observation of competent models also motivates teacher candidates to shift from observing to emulating their actions, and then gradually gain self-control until the point of reaching the independent level of self-regulation. In Zimmerman's description of the development of self-regulation, both the teacher (model) and the learner have tasks and responsibilities. The four levels of development are: observation, emulation, self-control, and self-regulation (see Table 2.4).

- *Observation* involves the learners' ability to perceive and retain the patterns of the behavior demonstrated by the teacher. The teacher models by thinking aloud, explaining the processes, and demonstrating and verbalizing concepts and processes. At this initial level, learners actively attend to the skills, strategies, methods, and processes displayed by the teacher.
- *Emulation* involves the learners' efforts to reproduce the patterns of behavior observed under the direct tutelage of the teacher. The teacher guides the learners while they attend to reproduce the observed behavior under direct supervision of the teacher who provides feedback. At this level, learners actively engage in imitation and simulation of the skills, strategies, methods, and processes displayed by the teacher.
- *Self-control* involves the learners' attempts to produce the observed behavior under minimal guidance from the teacher. The teacher remains available to provide feedback when it is needed with limited supervision while the students attempt to reproduce the behavior. At this level, learners actively employ skills to reproduce the observed behaviors according to their own competency and skills.
- *Self-regulation* involves the learners' attempt to reproduce the observed behaviors independently. Under similar situations and conditions and with teacher assistance only when it is absolutely necessary, the learner applies the newly acquired strategy. The teacher remains available to provide feedback when it is absolutely required or requested. They challenge their students to continue

adapting and transferring the newly learned skills to different settings and conditions. At this level, learners self-regulate their behavior, skills, and motivation in order to produce the observed behavior in different conditions and based on their own adaption and competence.

The phases of self-regulatory development are important to teacher training as a foundational approach for teaching children and adolescents (Randi 2004; Randi et al. 2011). Successful teachers routinely think aloud and verbalize their actions as they demonstrate a strategic approach to problem solving making sure their students are attentive to each and every action. They remain present and attentive to students who attempt to emulate what they have observed providing assistance as needed to move the student towards task completion. As students move into the self-control level and begin to take charge of planning their actions, teachers remain present to assist with task analysis and goal setting. At the self-regulation level, successful teachers support students as they attempt to apply learned behaviors to complete assigned tasks. They assist students to adapt their use of new strategies into new contexts based on their personal characteristics and self-efficacy beliefs.

Teacher candidates need self-regulated teacher educators (Dembo 2001). Caring teacher educators who focus on immediate and long-term goals, sustain a high level of self-efficacy, and have strong outcome expectancies provide students with vicarious learning experiences from good modeling. Their willingness to delay gratification and self-discipline while training teacher candidates is evidenced by their behaviors regarding their work and how frequently they provide feedback to their students. Teacher educators can be both role models and agents of transformation by demonstrating how they exercise influence over their own behavior, cognition, and environment. Although these patterns of behavior from teacher educators are important for all teacher candidates, it is essential for the development of self-regulation of teacher candidates who have experienced setbacks due to inadequate preparation as a result of attending schools in low socioeconomic settings, language barriers, and personal and family challenges (Randi 2004; Zimmerman 2002).

> Caring teacher educators who focus on immediate and long-term goals, sustain a high level of self-efficacy, and have strong outcome expectancies provide students with vicarious learning experiences from good modeling.

2.9 Research Evidence of the Developmental Phases of Self-regulation

Research studies have continually supported the developmental levels of self-regulation. Zimmerman and Kitsantas (2002) had college students observe a mastery or a coping model displaying writing revision skills and engage in emulation; the control group did not observe a model. Students who observed and emulated the coping model obtained higher self-regulatory writing skills than the other two groups. Zimmerman and Kitsantas (1997) trained high school students in dart throwing. After observing and emulating a model, students engaged in self-control and self-regulation. Shifting from a process to a product goal resulted in higher self-regulation and self-efficacy. McCaslin's (2001) approach of self-regulation focuses on empowering the individual through the development of an individual identity within the learning environment through a shift the burden of individual pursuit of goals to a shared responsibility. When faced with challenging tasks, interpersonal relationships can often impact success or failure. As students coordinate the multiple social worlds they can often go off track and experience great difficulty staying focused on their goals (Corno 1993). Once they realize from where they gain support, they can negotiate avenues of success with supportive assistant provided by the teacher. This interaction among teachers, students, and opportunities can be the link to eventual student self-regulation within a specific context (McCaslin and Good 1996). Help-seeking emphasizes that individuals' academic achievement can only be accomplished with accessible and available help providers.

In sum, in this chapter, we focus on social cognitive theory as an umbrella for the current case study with an emphasis on the importance of human agency and how learners acquire competencies, skills, dispositions, beliefs, and self-regulation. The theoretical framework and research of Bandura, Zimmerman, Corno, Winnie, Boekaerts, Pintrich, McCaslin, and Randi, among others, have informed and served and guided the current investigation. This chapter reports that self-regulated learning is one way in which aspiring teachers can be trained to become effective teaching professionals. The following chapter addresses the design of the case study and the methodology implemented to obtain data and holistically describes the setting in which the academic and teaching experience practices of four teacher candidates took place.

References

Ashton, P. (1985). Motivation and the teacher's sense of efficacy. *Research on motivation in education, 2,* 141–174.

Azevedo, R., Greene, J. A., & Moos, D. C. (2007). The effect of a human agent's external regulation upon college students hypermedia learning. *Metacognition and Learning, 2,* 67–87. doi: 10.1007/sl11409-007-9014-9.

Bandura, A. (1977). *Social learning theory.* Englewood Cliffs, NJ: Prentice Hall.

Bandura, A. (1997). *Self-efficacy: The exercise of control.* New York, NY: W. H. Freeman.

Bembenutty, H. (2006) *Preservice teachers' help-seeking tendencies and self-regulation of learning.* Paper presented at the annual meeting of the American Educational Research Association. San Francisco, CA.

Bembenutty, H., & Chen, P. P. (2005). Self-efficacy and delay of gratification. *Academic Exchange Quarterly, 9*(4), 78–86.

Bembenutty, H., Cleary, T. J., & Kitsantas, A. (2013). *Applications of self-regulated learning across diverse disciplines: A tribute to Barry J. Zimmerman.* Charlotte, NC: Information Age Publishing.

Bembenutty, H., & White, M. C. (2013). Academic performance and satisfaction with homework completion among college students. *Learning and Individual Differences, 24*, 83–88. doi:10.1016/j.lindif.2012.10.013.

Boekaerts, M. (1997). Self-regulated learning: A new concept embraced by researchers, policy makers, educators, teachers, and students. *Learning and Instruction, 7*(2), 161–186.

Boekaerts, M., & Niemivirta, M. (2000). Self-regulation in learning: Finding a balance between learning- and ego-protective goals. In M. Boekaerts, P. R Pintrich & M. Zeidner (Eds.), *Handbook of Self-Regulation* (pp. 417–450). San Diego, CA: Academic Press.

Boekaerts, M., Pintrich, P. R., & Zeidner, M. (Eds.). (2000). *Handbook of self-regulation*. San Diego, CA: Academic Press.

Clark, N. M. (2013). The use of self-regulation interventions in managing chronic disease. In H. Bembenutty, T. J. Cleary, & A. Kitsantas (Eds.), *Applications of self-regulated learning across diverse disciplines: A tribute to Barry J. Zimmerman* (pp. 417–444). Charlotte, NC: Information Age Publishing.

Clark, N. M., & Zimmerman, B. J. (2014). A social cognitive view of self-regulated learning about health. *Health Education & Behavior, 41*, 485–491. doi:10.1177/1090198114547512.

Corno, L. (1993). The best-laid plans: Modern conceptions of volition and educational research. *Educational Researcher, 22*(2), 14–22.

Dembo, M. H. (2001). Learning to teach is not enough: Future teachers also need to learn how to learn. *Teacher Education Quarterly, 28*(4), 23–35.

Kitsantas, A., & Dabbagh, N. (2010). *Learning to learn with integrative learning technologies (ILT): A practical guide for academic success*. Greenwich, CT: Information Age Publishing.

McCaslin, M. (2001). Self-regulated learning and academic achievement: A Vygotskian view. In B. Zimmerman & D. Schunk (Eds.), *Self-regulated learning and academic achievement: Theory, research and practice (pp143-168)*. New York: Springer.

McCaslin, M., & Good, T. (1996). The informal curriculum. In D. Berliner & R. Calfee (Eds.), *Handbook of Educational Psychology (pp84-151)*. Chicago: University of Chicago Press.

Nelson-Le Gall, S. (1981). Help-seeking: An understudied problem-solving skill in children. *Developmental Review, 1*(3), 224–246. doi:10.1016/0273-2297(81)90019-8.

Pajares, F. (1996). Self-efficacy beliefs in achievement settings. *Review of Educational Research, 66*, 543–578. doi:10.3102/00346543066004543.

Pintrich, P. R. (1999). The role of motivation in promoting and sustaining self-regulated learning. *International journal of educational research, 31*(6), 459–470.

Pintrich, P. R. (2000). The role of goal orientation in self-regulated learning. In M. Boekaerts, P. R. Pintrich, & M. Zeidner (Eds.), *Handbook of self-regulation* (pp. 451–502). San Diego, CA: Academic

Pintrich, P. R., & De Groot, E. V. (1990). Motivational and self-regulated learning components of classroom academic performance. *Journal of Educational Psychology, 82*(1), 33–40. doi:10.1037/0022-0663.82.1.33.

Pintrich, P. R., Smith, D. A. F., Garcia, T., & McKeachie, W. J. (1993). Reliability and predictive validity of the motivated strategies for learning questionnaire (MSLQ). *Educational and Psychological Measurement, 53*, 801–813.

Randi, J. (2004). Teachers as self-regulated learners. *Teachers College Record, 106*(9), 1825–1853.

Randi, J., Corno, L., & Johnson, E. (2011). Transitioning from college classroom to teaching career: Self-regulation in prospective teachers. *New Directions for Teaching and Learning, 126*, 89–98.

Schunk D. H., and Zimmerman, B. J. (2007). Influencing children's self-efficacy and self-regulation of reading and writing through modeling. *Reading & Writing Quarterly, 23*(1), 7–25. doi:10. 1080/10573560600837578

Tschannen-Moran, M., & Hoy, A. W. (2001). Teacher efficacy: Capturing an elusive construct. *Teaching and teacher education, 17*(7), 783–805.

Usher, E. L., & Pajares, F. (2008). Sources of self-efficacy in school: Critical review of the literature and future directions. *Review of Educational Research, 78,* 751–796. doi:10.3102/0034654308321456.

Vohs, K. D., & Baumeister, R. F. (Eds.). (2011). *Handbook of self-regulation: Research, theory, and applications* (2nd ed.). New York, NY: Guilford.

White, M. C. (2011). Predicting success in teacher certification testing: The role of academic help seeking. *International Journal of Educational and Psychological Assessment, 7*(1), 24–44.

White, M. C., & Bembenutty, H. (2013). Not all avoidance help seekers are created equal individual differences in adaptive and executive help seeking. *SAGE Open, 3*(2), 1–14. doi:10.1177/2158244013484916.

Winne, P. H. (1996). A metacognitive view of individual differences in self-regulated learning. *Learning and individual differences, 8*(4), 327–353.

Winne, P. H. (1997). Experimenting to bootstrap self-regulated learning. *Journal of Educational Psychology, 89,* 397–401.

Winne, P. H. (2001). Self-regulated learning viewed from models of information processing. In B. J. Zimmerman & D. H. Schunk (Eds.), *Self-regulated learning and academic achievement* (pp. 153–190). Mahwah, NJ: Lawrence Erlbaum Associates Inc.

Winne, P. H., & Perry, N. E. (2000). Measuring self-regulated learning. In M. Boekaerts, P. R. Pintrich & M. Zeidner (Eds.), *Handbook of Self-Regulation* (pp. 531–566). San Diego, CA: Academic Press.

Zimmerman, B. J. (2000). Attainment of self-regulation: A social cognitive perspective. In M. Boekaerts, P. R. Pintrich, & M. Zeidner (Eds.), *Handbook of self-regulation* (pp. 13–39). San Diego, CA: Academic Press.

Zimmerman, B. J. (2001). Theories of self-regulated learning and academic achievement: An overview and analysis. In B. J. Zimmerman & D. H. Schunk (Eds.), *Self-regulated learning and academic achievement: Theoretical perspectives* (2nd ed., pp. 1–37). Mahwah, NJ: Erlbaum.

Zimmerman, B. J. (2002). *Becoming a self-regulated learner: An overview: Theory into practice, 41*(2), 64–70.

Zimmerman, B. J., & Kitsantas, A. (1997). Developmental phases in self-regulation: Shifting from process goals to self-regulatory goals. *Journal of Educational Psychology, 91,* 241–250. doi:10.1037/0022-0663.89.1.29.

Zimmerman, B. J., & Kitsantas, A. (2002). Acquiring writing revision and self-regulatory skill through observation and emulation. *Journal of Educational Psychology, 94*(4), 660–668. doi:10.1037/0022-0663.94.4.660.

Zimmerman, B. J., & Schunk, D. H. (Eds.). (2011). *Handbook of self-regulation of learning and performance*. New York, NY: Routledge.

Chapter 3
Objectives and Methods

> During elementary education and secondary education, students
> are primarily guided by teachers and parents, for the most
> part take classes with the same peers, homework assignments
> are checked often, notes to parents are often sent about good
> academic progress, and children are to some extent protected
> from distractions and competing alternatives to education. On
> the other hand, at the post-secondary education level, students
> are expected to exercise control of their conduct, maintain
> motivation, develop plans for the future, exercise delay of
> gratification, and put into effect goals and learning strategies.
> Bembenutty (2011, pp. 5–6).

Abstract The chapter holistically describes the setting in which the academic and teaching experience practices of four teacher candidates took place. Data were collected during student teaching and clinical experiences in an urban setting from the perspective of social cognitive and self-regulation theoretical frameworks. This report is the first to follow four teacher candidates who would be considered unlikely teacher candidates with the present state standards for entrance into teacher education programs. As a result the pool of certified teachers who are best equipped to work in urban settings is decreasing, while the English language learning and minority population of pupils and parents is increasing. The faculty chose to focus on training in self-regulatory strategies for college entrants who aspire to be certified teachers but struggle to meet the academic and certification requirements. A description of the participants and institutional setting is evidence of a unique teacher preparation program fully aligned with the core values of the college.

Keywords Help seeking · Teacher educators · Self-regulation · Self-efficacy · Core values · Teaching experience

© The Author(s) 2015   29
H. Bembenutty et al., *Developing Self-regulation of Learning and Teaching Skills Among Teacher Candidates*, SpringerBriefs in Education,
DOI 10.1007/978-94-017-9950-8_3

3.1 General Objectives

We examine the academic and clinical experiences of four teacher candidates before and during their student teaching practicum in an urban setting. The researchers followed the students during several semesters of preparation and practicum to obtain evidence regarding the significance of their journeys and what their experiences meant to each of them. Each of the four students was interviewed individually, observed in the college classroom, and observed again in a designated elementary school classroom during student teaching placement. All of the teacher candidates responded to questionnaires assessing motivational beliefs, self-regulatory practices, beliefs about personal teaching capabilities, and opinions formed about the students whom they were teaching. In addition, a portfolio was developed by each teacher candidate, which reflected a self-assessment of individual growth as aspiring teachers.

The four teacher candidates' experiences were examined from the perspective of social cognitive theory and self-regulation theory. Based on the authors' years of professional teaching experiences as educational psychologists and clinical supervisors, the book will be the first in the literature to provide an integral account of the self-regulatory and motivational beliefs of four teacher candidates in a case study format. The book:

- Provides a direct account of the development of four teacher candidates before, during, and after their student teaching clinical experience.
- Focuses on contemporary educational theories to describe and interpret the training experiences of the four teacher candidates.
- Demonstrates the educational and psychological experiences that impacted their learning and teaching experiences.
- Provides directions for future research derived from the experience of these four teacher candidates.
- Provides directions for educational practices derived from the experiences of these four teacher candidates.

Successful learners engage in self-regulation of learning by using specific strategies to complete specific tasks (Zimmerman 1998). They exercise behavioral control when choosing and planning academic tasks and exercise self-control to maintain motivation and intention in the light of distracting alternatives (Bembenutty 2011). Self-regulation of learning is important not only for students in the general population but also for teacher candidates and inservice teachers. Similarly, as Bembenutty (2006) posited, like students, teachers and candidates need to be self-regulated individuals. Teacher candidates like other college students are often not predisposed to engage in self-regulation; they procrastinate, evidence maladaptive behavior, are pessimistic, and lack adaptive help seeking strategies. These students opt for immediate gratification rather than to delay gratification by putting more pleasurable activities before studying. In addition, they have a tendency to maintain low levels of self-efficacy beliefs that often undermine their capability and competence to perform designated and important teacher preparation tasks.

With regard to teacher candidates and help seeking, some teacher candidates in need of academic support are reluctant to seek help while others have the necessary qualities to actively seek the help required to overcome an instance of academic crisis.

With regard to teacher candidates and help seeking, some teacher candidates in need of academic support are reluctant to seek help while others have the necessary qualities to actively seek the help required to overcome an instance of academic crisis. One of those identified learning strategies that teacher candidates can use is adaptive help seeking (White 2011). *Help seeking* refers to the strategic self-regulatory ways in which learners obtain information from formal and informal sources in order to adapt and to secure knowledge acquisition and task completion (Karabenick 2004).

In an academic context, help seeking is related to delay of gratification. Bembenutty and Karabenick (1998) defined *delay of gratification* as learners' intentions to postpone immediately available rewards in order to obtain larger rewards temporally distant. Delay of gratification is important for self-regulation of learning (Bandura and Mischel 1965; Bembenutty 2007; Mischel 2014). Teacher candidates are often faced with more attractive alternatives than the necessary actions required to attain academic goals, in part, because they offer immediate gratification, in contrast to rewards for academic goals (e.g., grades, degrees, teacher certification) that are temporally remote. Delay of gratification is associated with students' use of learning strategies such as help seeking (Bembenutty and Karabenick 1998).

Teacher candidates' self-efficacy for learning is associated with both delay of gratification and help seeking because their beliefs in their capability to perform specific tasks determine whether or not they will take the time away from completing the task to seek help. In addition, self-efficacy for learning can also be associated with teacher self-efficacy for motivating students in their classrooms, teaching challenging students, and transferring content knowledge and learning skills to their students.

Self-regulation and motivation are essential components of learning practices for teacher candidates to succeed in urban education programs. The disparity in achievement experienced by students in high needs urban areas when compared with students who have significantly more economic resources has become a focal point in the field of education (Foote 2005). Many minority teacher candidates have significant deficiencies in arts and science skills which can be attributed to being underprepared (Vegas et al. 2001; McCabe 2000). Deficiencies in these areas can be remediated with appropriate instruction (Tobolowsky et al. 2005; Ley and Young 1998). As states implement tests for teacher certification with increasingly higher cut-off scores, there is concern that the number of minorities actually entering the classroom as teachers will decline significantly (Cochran-Smith and Zeichner 2010).

3.2 Two Major Objectives of the Study

The present case study has the following two major objectives: (1) to examine the association between the different self-regulatory skills and motivational beliefs of four teacher candidates during their student teaching clinical experience in an urban city, and (2) to examine the association between the their self-regulatory and motivational tendencies with their college training, lesson plan development and implementation, relationship with their students in the classroom, and reflection of their own learning and teaching preparation.

3.3 Educational Setting

The case study participants were drawn from a small, private college in an urban city. The college is nationally recognized for its ethnic, socio-economic, and cultural diversity among students and faculty. Anyone familiar with the core values of the college understands that it seeks to be academically excellent, globally engaged, intentionally diverse, socially relevant, and personally transforming.

The institutional goals can be linked to a social cognitive perspective of acquiring academic skills which proposes that social learning experiences can be planned and organized to accelerate self-regulatory development (Zimmerman and Schunk 1997). Social cognitive theory suggests that learning occurs through reciprocal interactions between personal, behavioral, and environmental factors (Schunk 2001). These domains are linked in human performance so that change to any of the domains will naturally impact the other. The core values of the institution emphasize the management of personal, environmental, and behavioral influences as a means to not only academic success but lifelong learning and achievement.

- *Alignment of Institutional Core Values with Self-regulation*: Teacher candidates are encouraged to focus on becoming capable, caring, and reflective professional educators equipped to serve communities locally, nationally, and internationally (see Table 3.1).
- *Alignment of Education Program with Self-regulation*: The conceptual framework reflects a set of expectations that guides the program. It focuses on the central aspects of the college goals and is integrated across and within all education programs. Four strands of competence provide the framework for each teacher candidate to understand the impact of culture in key areas of teacher education. The strands are interactive, with one continuously informing and shaping the other (see Table 3.2).

To some degree, college students often have difficulty balancing the social versus educational demands of the higher education experience (Zimmerman et al. 1994). One distinguishing characteristic between at risk and regular admission college students is the way they plan, organize, monitor, evaluate, and think about the learning process (Carr et al. 1991). Studies indicate a growing interest in the content of programs that facilitate students' transition into college. As noted in

Table 3.1   Alignment of institutional core values with self-regulation

Institutional core value	Description	Alignment to the self-regulation theory
Academically excellent	Pursuing academic excellence with an unassuming nature	Students are empowered to become independent and proactive learners by engaging in help seeking and self-monitoring strategies with the encouragement and support of faculty and administration (Zimmerman 1990)
Globally engaged	Fostering a global perspective within a multi-ethnic and multicultural academic community	Students are exposed and trained to access resources beyond the boundaries of the traditional college environment to achieve set goals. Provisions are made by instructors to encourage peers from diverse cultural backgrounds to form study groups and foster partnerships with students from other learning communities (Volet and Karabenick 2006)
Intentionally diverse	Providing educational access and support to motivated students from diverse socioeconomic backgrounds	Students are instructed to self-assess individual differences in learning, prior knowledge, and utilize sociocultural agents (e.g., teachers, peers) to succeed (Zimmerman 2004). The availability of both peer and expert tutors, study groups, and instructor support, provides underprepared students with access to learning opportunities and encouragement to be proactive in their own learning (Bembenutty et al. 2013)
Socially relevant	Preparing students to serve in educational and community building professions	Students are prepared for community building through self-monitoring and self-reflection while participating in field work and study opportunities in the USA and abroad (DiBenedetto and White 2013)
Personally transforming	Emphasizing the integration of many factors for individual transformation	Students admitted to the institution are required to become proactive learners through goal setting and defined outcome expectations (Zimmerman and Schunk 2004; Bandura 1997)

the case of the institution from which the participants were drawn, recent surveys indicate that approximately 70 % of American colleges and universities offer some type of first year supportive courses (Tobolowsky et al. 2005). To some degree, academic failure for these students may be explained by poor self-regulation (Young and Ley 2004). The college believes when learners are instructed in ways to regulate their social environment by seeking high quality sources, it is more likely that their motivation and behavior will improve (Paris and Paris 2001; Zimmerman et al. 1996; Zimmerman and Martinez-Pons 1990). For this reason, the institution offers several different types of workshops and courses to strengthen

Table 3.2 Alignment of education program with self-regulation

School of education core values	Description	Self-regulation theory application
Service	Understanding the impact of culture while stressing the importance of both the individual and group in a variety of cultures, contexts, and communities	Teacher candidates are trained to engage themselves, and consequently their students, in meaningful learning tasks as a means to develop self-efficacy. Challenging community based learning experiences require teacher candidates to independently set proximal goals, plan, perform, and self-evaluate their performance. When students perceive satisfactory goal progress, they feel capable of improving their skills; goal attainment, coupled with high self-efficacy, leads students to set new challenging goals (Schunk 1990)
Academics	Acquiring expertise in a chosen field of study, evidencing comprehension of best practices, and seeing the connection, or integration of content, theory, and clinical practice along with a strong liberal arts component	Choices are critical to goal setting and attribution. Intrinsic task interest encourages motivation and raises outcome expectations (Zimmerman 1990)
Leadership	Planning for continuous improvement linking the teacher candidates' shared goals, effective communication skills, and professional development to becoming models of excellence in teaching and learning practices	Prioritizing tasks and delaying gratification are essential to successful completion of the program. Students in the program are required to model self-regulatory behaviors which vicariously can impact their younger peers and future students (Bembenutty 2007)
Teaching	Developing pedagogical skills, which demonstrate reflection, planning, use of collaborative teaching strategies, and effective assessment. Effective teaching is a thoughtful practice that assesses and reflects on past performance and informs future practice	Students are evaluated on their use of strategies to self-monitor and evaluate their performance during and after presenting a lesson. The ability to reflect on one's performance and attribute success or failure to specific actions during the lesson is considered an important characteristic of a teacher who will model these behaviors for his/her students (Dembo 2001)

academic performance and help students manage knowing that without this type of support many students enrolled in the college could become discouraged with their progress and drop out.

The institution chose to add an urban extension some years ago seeking to provide inner city young people with access to higher education. One of the first programs promoted at the urban campus was a bachelor's degree in childhood education with accreditation for state certification. A key problem facing the teacher workforce across America is how to attract, prepare, and retain teachers in high poverty urban schools (Boyd et al. 2006). A primary place to seek teaching candidates from under represented populations is among those who already reside in a particular urban area and will effectively teach urban children (Haberman 2000). In order to tap this pool of potential minority teachers, educators must take into account the learning experiences of these teacher candidates prior to college. These students require programs that address their personal as well as their academic needs.

As evidenced in the biographies of the participants, many minority students are either first-generation college attendees or older students whose families have little or no prior experience with the demands of college. They are striving to be the first college graduates in their families (Gonzalez 1997). Although there are several, one important area of weakness that limits success in college, especially for minority students, is ineffective attempts to seek and obtain help (Caldwell and Siwatu 2003). The researchers surveyed pre-college initiative programs that were successful in transitioning under prepared high school students to higher education finding that along with interventions for developing cognitive learning skills minority students would benefit from training in social learning skills.

The college's enrollment reflects the population of most urban cities, providing an edge in developing a program that is effective for urban schools. Total enrollment at the institution for both the undergraduate and the graduate program is 3,369. The undergraduate program is the largest program with 2,157 students enrolled. Students can choose from 34 majors and study at either a residential campus or the urban campus.

The School of Education is accredited by the National Council for Accreditation of Teacher Education (NCATE) and is committed to preparing teacher candidates with practiced, research-based methodology. To fulfill these values, the faculty is committed to the preparation of teacher candidates who are capable of working effectively with diverse populations in a constantly changing global community.

The undergraduate teacher preparation programs train candidates to teach in the following areas: Early Childhood Education (Birth—Grade 2); Early Childhood/Childhood Education (Birth—Grade 6); Childhood Education (Grades 1–6); Adolescence Education with concentrations in English, Mathematics and Social Studies; and Music Education (K-12). Successful completion of the undergraduate programs leads to state initial certification.

Teachers trained at the college are required to master the core courses plus the specialization courses for the certification being sought. They are mentored as they gain command of the subject they plan to teach and are required to know a variety of methods and technologies to help students with individual differences. From the beginning, they observe and practice in designated clinical placements which are in urban educational settings. The program recognizes that transitioning from the role of student to teacher while maintaining the role of the learner provides teacher candidates with opportunities to take control of their own learning and engage in self-regulated learning (Randi 2004; Zeichner 1996). During their clinical experiences, teacher candidates work with highly effective urban education teachers who model for the teacher candidate *real time* knowledge, strategies, and self-regulation.

Clinical requirements are met by intentionally letting teacher candidates complete the required hours in their neighborhood schools or educational settings in high needs areas. Beginning with the first educational psychology course, students are placed in areas where teachers and principals have at risk children who require one to one attention in literacy and math in order to successfully complete the core requirement. Teacher candidates have also served after school programs by assisting with small group instruction, participating in community activities, and by providing assistance with homework assignments. In order to better meet the demands of the communities the education program serves, the education department invited clinical field partners to the college. The goal was to have a dialogue regarding their clinical partners' expectations of the students assigned to their learning environments, and as a result, they collaborated to develop a participant profile of the teacher candidates who chooses to work in low income and urban learning institutions that serve at risk students.

Work Study funds from the federal government have been designated to schools that are equipped to provide students with training from highly effective urban teaching professionals specifically in literacy development. One of the participants provided tutoring and classroom assistance to teachers whose students required one to one interventions to be academically successful. An additional clinical site requires bilingual (Spanish) administrators and teachers to meet the needs of their student and parent population. The college's partnership with this school has provided students enrolled in literacy methods classes a place to complete their clinical experience, enabling the participants to assist a young, energetic principal with the many projects she has implemented to have her school rated as one of the most successful in the city serving a primarily English language learning population.

As a result of their training and disposition to work in places where they are needed the most, the majority of the graduates from the School of Education have chosen to work in lower income schools. They often shared how well they have been prepared to teach in poorly resourced learning environments where children require the teacher be equipped with prior knowledge of the community and where they can demonstrate the core values of the institution.

3.4 A General Description of Participants

The teacher candidates involved in the study are not unique to today's undergraduate population. It is estimated that one third of the students who entered colleges and universities were underprepared or lacked the skills they needed to be successful

(Burd 1996; Morrissey 1994). In 1995, three fourths of the postsecondary institutions reported that incoming freshmen required at least one remedial or developmental reading, writing, or mathematics course. In 2010, 60 % of college entrants required remedial courses. The issue is no longer whether or not to accept underprepared college applicants, but how to identify and assist them. Arguments which support "open admission" include maximizing educational opportunity to give students a chance to show what they can do (Gleazer 1968).

One of the challenges to an institution which admits urban, underprepared students who come from low socioeconomic backgrounds is providing support in areas that will increase retention and graduation. There is an increased risk of failure for these students to meet the requirements to become teacher education candidates. Historically, the attrition rate among aspiring minority teachers due to failure on teacher certification tests of basic skills has been heavy (Cochran-Smith and Zeichner 2010). In the arena of teacher education, assessing help-seeking behavior would be one way to identify students who are not likely to take advantage of opportunities which would increase their likelihood of success.

As states implement tests for teacher certification with increasingly higher cut-off scores, we share the concern that the number of minorities actually entering the classroom as teachers will decline significantly (Cochran-Smith and Zeichner 2010). Important differences among racial and ethnic groups in the rates of success at each step along the path to teaching help explain why minority students are often unsuccessful on teacher certification exams which evaluate basic skills. Native American, Black, and Hispanic high school sophomores are less likely to obtain high school diplomas than are White or Asian American sophomores (Vegas et al. 2001). They are more likely to grow up in low-income families and attend low-quality schools than White youth. College entry rates for minorities are lower than Whites and Asian Americans. African Americans have a higher estimated probability of entering college than Hispanics or Native Americans.

It is not a mystery why the number of minorities who state their intention to enter teacher education programs dissipates by 50 % throughout the four to 5 year stint (Bennett 2002; Gonzalez 1997). When asked, minority teacher candidates have been able to identify program features that have a positive effect on recruitment, retention, and graduation into the teaching profession. One of the most significant components reported was an extension of support systems to attenuate the culture shock experienced by many first generation college attendees. Bennett (2002) concluded a new type of project design is needed beyond the standard structured remedial interventions usually offered to underprepared minority students. A more holistic view of minority students is needed to provide them with appropriate support.

All four teacher candidates were enrolled as full-time students. These students are representative of populations from low socio-economic status areas in a large urban city in a northeast state of the United States. All of the participants attended public high schools. In spite of the many challenges to their academic growth and development which include being educated in some of the lowest performing schools, each one was admitted to the college. Three of the four were required to take remedial courses before they could declare a major. Academic achievement at the college level was evaluated using GPA. Three of the four students achieved a 3.70 GPA while the fourth's GPA was 3.30. The age range for the four participants was 22–25.

All four students are bilingual (Spanish/English) with Spanish being the first language of the home and became the first to attend and graduate from college in their families. In addition, all four chose Childhood Education as a major. As they prepared for their student teaching, the teacher candidates were given opportunities to do their clinical and work study hours in bilingual schools with low SES populations.

The group shares some commonalities that brought them to the attention of the researchers. All four students are bilingual (Spanish/English) with Spanish being the first language of the home and became the first to attend and graduate from college in their families. In addition, all four chose Childhood Education as a major. As they prepared for their student teaching, the teacher candidates were given opportunities to do their clinical and work study hours in bilingual schools with low SES populations. They expressed a desire to teach in schools in the neighborhoods where they received their elementary education so they could bring their expertise in both teaching and cultural diversity to failing schools.

Specific to these participants is their choice to seek admission to the School of Education at the urban campus with the intention to graduate with the credentials required to become a state certified teacher. Both the institution and the School of Education provide ongoing support to students who have experienced academic challenges either in high school or at other postsecondary institutions by incorporating research based methods and assessments into the curriculum.

The institution is committed to a strong retention rate, and acknowledges the challenges coupled with admitting underprepared students. For this reason, close monitoring of teacher education candidates who are in the pipeline for state certification and graduation is critical to the growth and development of the institution. Serious consideration is given to research studies which support efforts to retain students in a program or the college at large. As a result, the case study participants, as well as many of their colleagues, were, and continue to be, closely monitored through voluntary participation in research studies, ongoing assessments, and strategic mentoring. Close contact is maintained while teacher candidates are enrolled in the college, even if they leave the certification track. Strong ties with the alumni help the faculty receive feedback regarding current educational practices in a variety of educational settings as well as provide a professional base of mentors for the current population of teacher candidates.

Table 3.3 Demographics for students

Variables	Chris	Maria	Angela	Jaime
Race/Ethnicity	Hispanic	Hispanic	Hispanic	Hispanic
Gender	Male	Female	Female	Female
Socioeconomic status	Low	Low	Low	Low
Age	25	25	26	22
High school GPA	1.40	2.10	2.50	3.20
Languages spoken	English/Spanish	English/Spanish	English/Spanish	English/Spanish
Initial admission status	Conditional	Conditional	Conditional	Regular
English as a second language	Yes	Yes	Yes	Yes
LAST score	246	233	235	233
ATS-W score	236	258	250	240
CST score	228	222	215	233
College GPA	3.38	2.75	3.41	3.71
Program of study	Elementary	Elementary	Elementary	Elementary
Work experience	Work study	Office	Work study	Retail
Current position 2 years after graduation	Teaches 2nd grade at a public school and obtained a master's in TESOL. December 2012	Teaches 4th grade students at a charter school and obtained a master's in Special Education. December 2012	Works as a legal assistant criminal justice and works to obtain a TESOL certification at a research university and maintains private tutoring	Teaches 2nd grade at a religious academy and obtained a master's in education December 2012

The four teacher candidates featured in the case study were among many aspiring teacher candidates for whom it was initially acknowledged that their high school GPA and scores from a test measuring basic skills (Liberal Arts & Sciences Test) placed them in jeopardy of not meeting the requirements to be admitted to the School of Education at the end of their sophomore year. In addition, they were part of an investigation of their use of help seeking as a self-regulatory strategy for evidence of how this group of aspiring teacher candidates would participate in test preparation workshops that could help them to gain entry into a challenging teacher education program. The participants were drawn from a larger population of entry level teacher candidates following an initial assessment of their help-seeking behaviors while preparing for the first of three state certification exams. As they progressed in the program, data were collected relating to the development of self-regulatory strategies beyond the passing of state exams to success in student teaching.

Initially, data were collected relating the use of help-seeking as a self-regulation strategy to pass state certification exams and succeed in student teaching. Following the passing of the first teacher certification exam, two faculty members continued to statistically track the progress of several of their teacher candidates in fulfilling their goals to graduate as fully certified teachers. The case study came about as a result of the faculty members' desire to use extended data to support their beliefs that the self-regulatory strategy of help seeking was closely related to their students' successful completion of the teacher education program (see Table 3.3).

3.5 Biographies of Participants During Data Collection

- **Chris (1)** is a Puerto Rican, 25 year old male who is fluent in both English and Spanish. In his entire family, he is the first person to graduate from both high school and college, and although there was emotional support from his grandmother, the family could not provide financial resources. Initially, Chris struggled to pass the first of three certification exams, which is a test of basic skills upon entry to college. Financial aid in the form of work study compensation enabled Chris to be employed in a school with a significant population of English language learners. While he pursued a Bachelor's degree, he was able to work 25 h a week and graduate with a 3.40 GPA majoring in Childhood Education. As a result of his strong performance as student teacher in a challenging learning environment, the principal recommended Chris for a 2nd grade teaching position in a neighboring school.
- **Angela (2)** is a 26 year old female who was born in the Dominican Republic. She migrated with her family to the United States when she was 8 years old. She considers her first language to be Spanish and English as a second language. She is proficient in speaking and reading both languages. As the first one in her family to graduate from high school and then attend college, she received emotional and financial support from her family. However, while she pursued a Bachelor's degree with a major in Childhood Education, her family moved to out of the state, which made the commute very time consuming and stressful.

Nevertheless, she completed her degree in 2011 and is now enrolled in a graduate program to obtain a Master's in Literacy. Angela's desire to work with children has resulted in serving as a volunteer tutor for the public school in her area and working with struggling students as a home tutor.

- **Jaime (3)** is a 22 old female whose parents were born in the Dominican Republic. She is fluent in both English and Spanish. She was able to maintain a full course load and work part time while she earned a Bachelor's degree majoring in Childhood Education. Financial aid in the form of work study compensation enabled Jaime to be employed in a school with a significant English Language Learners (ELL) population. She graduated with a GPA of 3.65 and is enrolled in a graduate program to obtain a Master's degree in Special Education to be completed in December of 2012. In addition, she is employed as a kindergarten teacher in a private school located in a middle class community but serving a diverse population of students from outside the area.

- **Maria (4)** is a Puerto Rican, 25 year old female who is fluent in both English and Spanish. She reports that attending college for her was a struggle due to financial and family pressures. As the first one in her family to attend college, she was required to work full time due to financial needs and support her family during times of crises. In order to qualify for financial aid, she carried a full load of courses and often took overloads to obtain a Bachelor's degree majoring in Childhood Education. These factors contributed to her 2.90 GPA, which is not reflective of her ability, but of multiple stressors beyond her control. As a result of her growth and development as a self-regulated learner, this participant chose to enter graduate school and pursue a Master's degree in Special Education. In addition, she was employed by the public school system as a substitute teacher until she was hired as an assistant teacher in a special education classroom by a charter school in an urban community. Upon completion of her Master's degree and state certification, she will become a lead teacher in the same setting.

Overall, this chapter describes the setting in which the learning and teaching experience of four aspiring teachers took place and informed that data were collected in an urban setting in which students were exposed to components of the self-regulation theory. Four teacher candidates were followed over 4 years since their entrance into teacher education programs. The following chapter describes the clinical experiences of the teacher candidates while they were observed in schools.

References

Bandura, A. (1997). *Self-efficacy: The exercise of control.* New York, NY: W. H. Freeman.

Bandura, A., & Mischel, W. (1965). Modifications of self-imposed delay of reward through exposure to live and symbolic models. *Journal of Personality and Social Psychology, 2,* 698–705. doi:10.1037/h0022655.

Bembenutty, H. (2006, April). *Preservice teachers' help-seeking tendencies and self-regulation of learning.* Paper Presented at the Annual Meeting of the American Educational Research Association, San Francisco, CA.

Bembenutty, H. (2007). Self-regulation of learning and academic delay of gratification: Gender and ethnic differences among college students. *Journal of Advanced Academics, 18*(4), 586–616.

Bembenutty, H. (2011). Meaningful and maladaptive homework practices: The role of self-efficacy and self-regulation. *Journal of Advanced Academics, 22*(3), 448–473. doi:10.1177/193 2202X1102200304.

Bembenutty, H., Cleary, T. J., & Kitsantas, A. (2013). *Applications of self-regulated learning across diverse disciplines: A tribute to Barry J. Zimmerman*. Charlotte, NC: Information Age Publishing.

Bembenutty, H., & Karabenick, S. A. (1998). Academic delay of gratification. *Learning and Individual Differences, 10*, 329–346. doi:10.1016/S1041-6080(99)80126-5.

Bennett, C. (2002). Enhancing ethnic diversity at a big ten university through project TEAM: A case study in teacher education. *Educational Researcher, 31*(2), 21–29.

Boyd, D., Grossman, P., Lankford, H., Loeb, S., Michelli, N., & Wyckoff, J. (2006). Complex by design: Investigating pathways into teaching in New York City schools. *Journal of Teacher Education, 57*, 155–166).

Burd, S. (1996). Neediest students face threat of narrowed access. *Chronicle of higher education, 42*(31), A39–A45.

Caldwell, L. D., & Siwatu, K. O. (2003). Promoting academic persistence in African American and Latino high school students: The educational navigation skills seminar. *High School Journal, 87*, 30–38.

Carr, M., Borkowski, J. G., & Maxwell, S. E. (1991). Motivational components of under achievement. *Developmental Psychology, 27*, 108–118.

Cochran-Smith, M., & Zeichner, K. M. (Eds.). (2010). *Studying teacher education: The report of the AERA panel on research and teacher education*. New York, NY: Routledge.

Dembo, M. H. (2001). Learning to teach is not enough: Future teachers also need to learn how to learn. *Teacher Education Quarterly, 28*(4), 23–35.

DiBenedetto, M. K., & White, M. C. (2013). Applying the model of development of self-regulatory competence to mentoring. In H. Bembenutty, T. J. Cleary, & A. Kitsantas (Eds.), *Applications of self-regulated learning across diverse disciplines: A tribute to Barry J. Zimmerman* (pp. 445–472). Charlotte, NC: Information Age Publishing.

Foote, C. J. (2005). The challenge and potential of high-need urban education. *The Journal of Negro Education, 74*(4), 371–381.

Gleazer, E. J. (1968). *This is the community college*. Boston, MA: Houghton-Mifflin.

Gonzalez, J. (1997). Recruiting and training minority teachers: Student views of the preservice program. *Equity & Excellence in Education, 30*(1), 56–64.

Haberman, M. (2000). Increasing the number of high-quality African American teachers in urban schools. *Journal of Instructional Psychology, 26*, 208–212.

Karabenick, S. A. (2004). Perceived achievement goal structure and college student help seeking. *Journal of Educational Psychology, 96*, 569–581.

Ley, K., & Young, D. (1998). Self-regulation in underprepared (developmental) and regular admission college students. *Contemporary Educational Psychology, 23*, 42–64.

McCabe, R. H. (2000). *No one to waste: A report to public decision-makers and community college leaders*. Washington, DC: Community College Press.

Mischel, W. (2014). *The marshmallow test: Mastering self-control*. New York, NY: Little, Brown and Company.

Morrissey, M. (1994). Colleges increasing support to help underprepared students succeed. *Counseling Today, 1*, 6.

Paris, S. G., & Paris, A. H. (2001). Classroom applications of research on self-regulated learning. *Educational Psychologist, 36*(2), 89–101. doi:10.1207/S15326985EP3602_4.

Randi, J. (2004). Teachers as self-regulated learners. *Teachers College Record, 106*(9), 1825–1853.

Schunk, D. H. (1990). Goal setting and self-efficacy during self-regulated learning. *Educational Psychologist, 25*, 71–86. doi:10.1207/s15326985ep2501_6.

Schunk, D. H. (2001). Social cognitive theory and self-regulated learning. In B. J. Zimmerman & D. H. Schunk (Eds.), *Self-regulated learning and academic achievement: Theoretical perspectives* (pp. 125–152). Mahwah, NJ: Lawrence Erlbaum Associates.

Tobolowsky, B. F., Mamrick, M., & Cox, B. E. (2005). *The 2003 national survey of first-year seminars: Continuing innovations in the collegiate curriculum.* Columbia, SC: University of South Carolina, National Resource Center for the First-Year Experience and Students in Transition.

Vegas, E., Murnana, R. I., & Willett, J. B. (2001). From high school to teaching: Many steps, who makes it? *Teachers College Record, 103*(3), 427–449.

Volet, S., & Karabenick, S. A. (2006). Help Seeking in Cultural Context. In S. A. Karabenick & R. S. Newman (Eds.), *Help seeking in academic setting: Goals, groups, and contexts* (pp. 117–150). Mahwah, NJ: Lawrence Erlbaum Associates Publishers.

White, M. C. (2011). Predicting success in teacher certification testing: The role of academic help seeking. *International Journal of Educational and Psychological Assessment, 7*(1), 24–44.

Young, D., & Ley, K. (2004). Self-regulation support offered by developmental educators. *Journal of Developmental Education, 27*, 2–10.

Zeichner, K. (1996). Designing educative practicum experiences. In K. Zeichner, S. Melnick, & M. L. Gomez (Eds.), *Current reforms in preservice education* (pp. 215–234). New York: Teacher's College Press.

Zimmerman, B. J. (1990). Self-regulated learning and academic achievement: An overview. *Educational Psychologist, 25*(1), 3–17.

Zimmerman, B. J. (1998). Developing self-fulfilling cycles of academic regulation: An analysis of exemplary instructional models. In D. H. Schunk & B. J. Zimmerman (Eds.), *Self-regulated learning: From teaching to self-reflective practice* (pp. 1–19). New York, NY: Guilford Press.

Zimmerman, B. J. (2004). Sociocultural influence and students' development of academic self-regulation: A social-cognitive perspective. In D. M. McInerney & S. van Etten (Eds.), *Big theories revisited: research on sociocultural influences on motivation and learning* (pp. 139–164). Greenwich, CT: Information Age Publishing.

Zimmerman, B. J., Bonner, S., & Kovach, R. (1996). *Developing self-regulated learners: Beyond achievement to self-efficacy.* Washington, DC: American Psychological Association. doi:10.1037/10213-000.

Zimmerman, B. J., Greenberg, D., & Weinstein, C. E. (1994). Self-regulating academic study time: A strategy approach. In D. H. Schunk & B. J. Zimmerman (Eds.), *Self-regulation of learning and performance* (pp. 181–202). NJ: Erlbaum.

Zimmerman, B. J., & Martinez-Pons, M. (1990). Student differences in self-regulated learning: Relating grade, sex, and giftedness to SE and strategy use. *Journal of Educational Psychology, 82*(1), 51–59. doi:10.1037/0022-0663.82.1.51.

Zimmerman, B. J., & Schunk, D. H. (1997). Social origins of self-regulatory competence. *Educational psychologist, 34*(4), 195–209.

Zimmerman, B. J., & Schunk, D. (2004). Self-regulating process and outcomes: A social cognitive perspective. In D. Y. Dai & R. J. Sternberg (Eds.), *Motivation, emotion, and cognition: Perspectives on intellectual development and functioning* (pp. 323–349). Mahweh, NJ: Erlbaum.

Chapter 4
School Observations and Classroom Experience

> *In our attempt to give underprepared minority teacher candidates the opportunity to become certified teachers, we must look for indicators of future success. Measurement of the important self-regulatory strategy of help seeking is one way to predetermine if an aspiring teacher will use the resources made available by teacher education programs and other supportive groups to assist them in passing a test of basic skills. It is suggested that the scales can be used by teacher education programs to evaluate aspiring teachers' potential to pass the teacher certification exams by accounting for his/ her disposition to use appropriate means to when preparing for state certification exams.*
>
> White (2011, p. 15).

Abstract This chapter describes the clinical experiences of four teacher candidates while they were completing student teaching in a program with a heavy emphasis on help seeking and delay of gratification as two self-regulated learning strategies and it describes a set of classroom observations. The institution's core values influence every aspect of teacher preparation including how student teaching placements are selected. Teacher candidates should be able to thrive in learning environments with diverse populations in urban settings, but in addition, be challenged to work with parents and educators whose backgrounds and life experiences are unfamiliar. Both public and private school settings provided venues for clinical experiences and the completion of the Teacher Work Sample. In addition, teacher candidates were observed in these settings using reliable instruments constructed to measure help seeking before, during, and after a lesson was planned and delivered. The findings across all teacher candidates evidence behaviors during their individual clinical experiences that can be attributed to self-regulatory practices. Engagement in self-monitoring and self-evaluation enabled teacher candidates to attribute success and failure to specific areas of weakness or strength.

Keywords Observation · Assessment · Self-regulation · Help seeking · Teachers · Self-efficacy

H. Bembenutty et al., *Developing Self-regulation of Learning and Teaching Skills Among Teacher Candidates*, SpringerBriefs in Education,
DOI 10.1007/978-94-017-9950-8_4

The School of Education requires teacher candidates to devote their efforts and time to the student teaching segment of their teacher preparation program and not be employed outside the institution or involved in time consuming extra-curricular activities. Although it can be a financial hardship, this standard has been consistently applied and where necessary, financial assistance, although minimal, has been provided through work-study employment or scholarships. In addition, while student teaching, teacher candidates are encouraged to not take additional courses beyond the Senior Seminar. In the case of these particular teacher candidates, exceptions were made due to financial constraints. They were permitted to take the courses required to complete their degrees and graduate at the end of their student teaching semester. Returning to the college for another semester would have placed them in further debt and was a significant financial challenge for all four participants (Zapata 1988).

4.1 Observation of Student Teachers

The four teacher candidates were observed for indicators that could be attributed to self-regulatory practices. Specifically, the candidates were observed during individual clinical hours for evidence of help seeking, self-efficacy, classroom management, attention to diverse learners, differentiated instruction, content knowledge, and use of self-regulatory learning strategies. The observers were two experienced faculty members with more than 20 years of school and clinical-related educational experiences and teaching credentials. They were familiar with these four students from both classroom and clinical perspectives serving them as both supervisors and mentors (see Appendixes A–D).

Preparing both culturally responsive and highly qualified teachers is a significant goal of the teacher education program. The program is responsible for preparing future teachers that promote meaningful learning experiences for a diverse population of students regardless of race, gender, socio-economic background, and ethnicity or language differences.

4.2 Rationale for Placement

The four teacher candidates were placed in urban schools in the northeastern part of the United States. Critical to the decision making process that guides the placement of student teachers is aligning their abilities and skills with selected learning environments. Two considerations must be equally weighed, first that the school and classroom will benefit from the teacher candidate's participation and second, that the professionalism and standards of the school meet the criteria to foster the student teacher's individual growth and development as a teacher (Koerner et al. 2002). A shared commitment to the core values of both the institution and the School of Education was the motivation for placing three of the students in a school with a strong bilingual and English as a Second Language program.

Preparing both culturally responsive and highly qualified teachers is a significant goal of the teacher education program. The program is responsible for preparing future teachers that promote meaningful learning experiences for a diverse population of students regardless of race, gender, socio-economic background, and ethnicity or language differences. Remaining committed to the core value of global engagement, motivated the placement of the fourth student into a private school setting. Not only should teacher candidates be able to thrive in learning environments with diverse populations in an urban setting, but in addition, be challenged to work with parents and educators whose backgrounds and life experiences are unfamiliar and challenge equilibrium.

Both the challenge and the commitment center upon the goal to prepare teachers who will ensure equity of opportunity for all students. From early on in the program, teacher candidates are given the opportunity to practice their professional development in school districts that have diverse populations or learning environments that provide exposure to new and unfamiliar territory. Through participation in all types of educational arenas, the teacher candidate is expected to acquire an understanding of not only cultural and ethnic differences, but become prepared to address the needs of students from differing socioeconomic, developmental, cognitive and motivational levels. The long-term goal is to prepare a teacher who is equipped to generate a learning environment where diversity is recognized, incorporated, valued, and celebrated. As a result, under the guidance of a highly qualified teacher, individual differences do not negatively impact students striving to reach their full potential.

The placement of teacher candidates is aligned with recommendations made by the local department of education to each teacher candidate in a handbook. Student teachers placed in public schools are given the opportunity to gain hands-on experience with a diverse student population. The placement decision for three of the four teacher candidates also included using their bilingual proficiencies. Schools in high needs urban communities often need translators for the many parents who do not speak English. Students who are English language learners (ELL) often are placed in classrooms where the teacher is proficient only in English, thus creating a gap between the home and school. The college, through the placement of three teacher candidates, was able to provide a service to the larger community beyond the in-school setting (Ramirez 2003).

4.3 School: Public

The mission of the principal, teachers, staff, and parents of the public school where three of the four teacher candidates were placed for student teaching is to prepare students who will embrace education and become lifelong learners. Their goal is that everyone attains the essential knowledge and skills necessary to enable them to become exemplary citizens. A strong emphasis is placed on teamwork to achieve the highest standards. The progress report for the school year 2010–2011 noted an overall grade of "B" scoring in the 41st percentile when compared with other schools in the same city. The strongest score was in the area of school environment, which measures student attendance and surveys the school community to rate academic expectations, safety and respect, communication, and engagement. Once considered a failing school, the current principal has been able to create a learning environment in which teachers, parents, and students feel comfortable.

The weakest areas of performance for students enrolled in the school are in student performance, measured by improvement on state tests in English and Math when compared with students who started at the same level. The school provides remedial and enrichment activities for all students by inviting participation in programs which are offered both after school and on Saturdays. The English as a Second Language program has become a model for other urban schools due to the significant progress made by their students. Students with special needs are educated in diverse settings, which include both integrated and self-contained classes. One special education class is bilingual in English and Spanish.

4.4 School: Private

The fourth teacher candidate was placed in a private school known for its academic excellence, secure environment, and strong values. Situated in a district with highly rated public schools, the population of students is drawn from areas a significant distance beyond the surrounding middle class community. Small and multiage classes guarantee individual attention and advanced learning opportunities. The students' scores rank consistently above the national average on standardized tests. Enrichment programs include religion, computer education, foreign language, sports, and music.

The decision to place the fourth teacher candidate in this private setting was based on the college partnership with the school, the diverse population of students, and proximity to the candidate's home. In addition, there were many indications that the teacher candidate would benefit from working in a multiage learning environment that would challenge the candidate's content knowledge and pedagogy.

4.5 Senior Teaching Seminar Assignment

The student teaching seminar provides teacher candidates with a forum to discuss and develop a portfolio, the Teacher Work Sample (TWS), that reflects how their teaching impacts learning in an elementary school classroom. The construction of the TWS requires each teacher candidate to collect and use appropriate data to measure the outcome from his or her teaching efforts on the academic achievement of students during clinical practicum. In addition, the TWS provides the teacher candidates with data that can be used for reflective evaluations of their teaching and learning process (Kohler et al. 2008).

As part of their TWS, teacher candidates design an assessment plan to monitor student progress towards set learning objectives(s). They are trained to use multiple assessment modes that are aligned with task specific learning objectives to assess student learning before, during, and after instruction. The assessments chosen to measure student learning may include performance-based tasks, paper-and-pencil tasks, or personal communication. Teacher candidates are then asked to describe why each assessment is appropriate for measuring learning progress and outcomes.

Each learning objective requires assessments to judge student performance, the format of each assessment, and adaptations of the assessments for the individual needs of students based on pre-assessment and contextual factors. The purpose of this overview is to depict the alignment between learning objectives and assessments and to show adaptations to meet the individual needs of students or contextual factors. Teacher candidates are encouraged to use visual organizers, such as tables, outlines or other means to make the assessment plan clear.

During their clinical placements and while participating in Senior Seminar, the teacher candidates were observed to identify indications of engagement in self-regulation. Further observations to evaluate behaviors that evidence the use of help seeking as a self-regulatory strategy were conducted throughout each Senior Seminar meeting, and before, during, and after instruction. The four teacher candidates were observed during individual clinical experiences for indicators which could be attributed to the self-regulatory practices of the student teacher, specifically help seeking, self-efficacy, classroom management, attention to diverse learners, differentiated instruction, content knowledge, and use of self-regulatory learning strategies (Boekaerts and Corno 2005). The observers were two experienced instructors with more than 20 years of teaching credentials who know the students and the classroom settings.

Reliable protocols were developed by the researchers to guide the field observations. The protocols contain several assessment instruments specifying key actions and phrases to identify help seeking, self-efficacy, classroom management, and attention to diverse learners, differentiated instruction, content knowledge, and use of self-regulatory learning strategies. The total observation was carried out in three phases that occurred before, during, and following the presentation of a lesson to a group of students.

Phase one included data regarding the lesson about to be presented that could be collected up until 10 min before classroom observation. Any interactions regarding the planning of the lesson between the observers and teacher candidates prior to delivery of the lesson was noted. Data for phase two was collected during the classroom observation of the lesson, which is further described in the next paragraph. Phase three data were collected 10 min following the observation, during the debriefing of the delivered lesson in a planned face to face meeting between the observers and the teacher candidates. During the debriefing, the observers provided a reflection of the teacher candidate's performance that served as a means of assessing how the feedback was received.

The instruments for phase two were specifically designed for use in a clinical setting to assess instructional design, level of interactions between teacher candidates and their students, psychological approaches to teaching and learning, and content knowledge behavior in real time (Shulman 1987). The observers used only the provided key actions and phrases to identify teacher candidates' behavior. Direct observation began at the moment the teacher candidate made a statement that reflected the intention of beginning the lesson and took charge of the classroom. Evidence was retrieved during the instructional segment, guided practice, and the lesson summary. The observers collected data related to any overt behavior of the student teacher, which could be attributed to specific help-seeking goals, use of self-regulatory strategies, and specific conditions that encouraged self-regulation. Each candidate was observed three times in an elementary school setting.

4.6 Observation of Teacher Candidates

4.6.1 Chris

Chris was observed in a general education third grade classroom with 17 students, six boys and eleven girls. None of the students in the classroom had Individuated Educational Plans for special education services; however, one boy received in-school counseling. Academically, four of the students were performing above grade level, ten students were performing on grade level, and three students were performing below grade level in mathematics and reading. For both observations, Chris was consistently on task and evidenced a high level of professional development.

The observed lesson began with the lead teacher providing a short period of instruction for the whole group with Chris assisting. Evidence of cooperative teaching was observed, and Chris fulfilled his role whether he was in the lead or not. Although confident in the literacy lesson he had planned, Chris consistently took cues from the head teacher to self-monitor during the lesson. There was clear evidence of help seeking in the questions posed by the student teacher to the head teacher and in the way he received correction. In addition, he used a modeling technique to encourage participation amongst the third graders. He often used sticky notes to respond to students' questions giving them hints to encourage further investigation to arrive at the answer independently. Evidence of self-efficacy was demonstrated through the teacher candidate's level of confidence in the content area of the lesson and in his ability to interact appropriately with his cooperating teacher and the students while being observed by his professors.

4.6.2 Angela

Angela was observed in a third grade bilingual class preparing for the third grade state English Language Arts (ELA) exam. The cooperating teacher was a state certified common branches teacher who noted to the observers her significant confidence in Angela's bilingual proficiencies. The class included fourteen students from homes in which Spanish were the first language. Thirteen students were originally from Mexico and one student was from the Dominican Republic. There were eight males and six females, ages ranged from eight to ten. Two students were repeating the third grade. Three students received special education services through Individualized Educational Plans (IEP), two received speech therapy, and one received occupational therapy.

One problem noted by the teacher was the amount of English language learning lost as a result of the students being in Spanish speaking monolingual environments when not in school. The students were required to take the ELA assessment for all third graders, not the English as a Second Language Achievement Tests. This population of students often became discouraged due to failure on these state exams due to limited English proficiency and practice. One area of significant stress for these students is preparing for the essay section of the ELA.

Evidence of help seeking was observed when this teacher candidate met with her supervisor for feedback on her planning prior to presenting lessons. She gave every indication prior to the lesson that she wanted the students to be successful and began to practice self-regulation by setting proximal goals for each teaching segment. During the lesson, the teacher candidate remained in charge, yet often invited and reflected on feedback from the cooperating teacher before moving from one task to another. She self-monitored by taking the time to consult her notes and monitored the progress of her students to be sure she was spending the appropriate time on task. The students were often encouraged to be proactive and learn from each other while waiting for a response to posed questions. The teacher candidate modeled help seeking by directly asking the cooperating teacher questions and using the responses to move the class forward. She encouraged the students to provide "hints" for each other rather than answers.

4.6.3 Jaime

Jaime was observed in a first grade general education classroom. The population of twenty students included twelve boys and eight girls. None of the students in the classroom received special education services. The teacher candidate exhibited a great deal of confidence moving through her lessons quickly. However, because of the fast pace she often missed cues from the cooperating teacher that, if followed, could have improved both the presentation and student learning. Often, it was a challenge to maintain the interests of the students.

> Strategic planning and consistent interaction with the lead teacher helped this teacher candidate prepare for the challenges that can arise when teaching in this type of learning environment. The teacher candidate evidenced help seeking when she sought assistance from both the cooperating teacher and the clinical supervisor during the planning stage of the lesson.

During the first observation, it was evident to each observer that Jaime did not always demonstrate self-monitoring. As a result, she had difficulty monitoring her performance, apparently unaware of the errors in presentation that could have been easily avoided and corrected if she had been cognizant of the lead teacher's subtle attempts to assist. It was apparent that Jaime focused all of her attention on the lesson she had planned and did not evidence self-monitoring during the performance stage or a need to revise her goals. During a debriefing, she was able to self-evaluate and set more realistic and specific goals that were clearly evidenced in the next lesson. The second observation provided evidence of her ability to set proximal goals, and maintain a level of self-monitoring, and when reflecting on her own performance as well as her students, she reset her goals to meet the needs of the students.

4.6.4 Maria

Maria was observed in a multiage classroom of fifth and sixth graders, eighteen boys and four girls. Two students received special education services. Strategic planning and consistent interaction with the lead teacher helped this teacher candidate prepare for the challenges that can arise when teaching in this type of learning environment. The teacher candidate evidenced help seeking when she sought assistance from both the cooperating teacher and the clinical supervisor during the planning stage of the lesson.

As a result of self-monitoring, her level of awareness was raised and she detected some difficulty during the lesson. As a result, she enlisted the support of the lead teacher as she remained focused on the student's task engagement. Although she took the lead, she self-monitored and sought feedback from the cooperating teacher. These strategic behaviors resulted in adjustments to the teaching and learning process. In addition, the lesson included the opportunities for students to set goals and self-monitor. When the work could not be done independently, students were encouraged to use strategies and resources provided by the student teacher, but not provided with the answer.

4.7 Findings Across All Teacher Candidates

All four teacher candidates evidenced behaviors during their individual clinical experiences that can be attributed to self-regulatory practices. Initially, for three of the four candidates, help seeking was part of the planning, performance, and reflection phases of each task that eventually culminated in a lesson plan. For the fourth candidate, help seeking became a strategic tool after reflecting on the first performance. Key to the successful presentation of lesson plans for all four teacher candidates was the ability to reflect on performance of a specific part of the presentation, self-evaluate, and reset goals for the next teaching opportunity (Gay and Kirkland 2003). The teacher candidate's engagement in self-monitoring and self-evaluation enabled them to attribute success or failure of a lesson presentation to specific areas of weakness or strength.

References

Boekaerts, M., & Corno, L. (2005). Self-regulation in the classroom: A perspective on assessment and intervention. *Applied Psychology, 54*(2), 199–231.

Gay, G., & Kirkland, K. (2003). Developing cultural critical consciousness and self-reflection in preservice teacher education. *Theory into Practice, 42*(3), 181–187.

Koerner, M., Rust, F. O. C., & Baumgartner, F. (2002). Exploring roles in student teaching placements. *Teacher Education Quarterly, 29*(2), 35–58.

Kohler, F., Henning, J. E., & Usma-Wilches, J. (2008). Preparing preservice teachers to make instructional decisions: An examination of data from the teacher work sample. *Teaching and Teacher Education, 24*(8), 2108–2117.

Ramirez, A. F. (2003). Dismay and disappointment: Parental involvement of Latino immigrant parents. *The Urban Review, 35*(2), 93–110.

Shulman, L. S. (1987). Assessment for teaching: An initiative for the profession. *Phi Delta Kappan, 69*, 38–44.

White, M. C. (2011). Predicting success in teacher certification testing: The role of academic help seeking. *International Journal of Educational and Psychological Assessment, 7*(1), 24–44.

Zapata, J. T. (1988). Early identification and recruitment of his panic teacher candidates. *Journal of Teacher Education, 39*(1), 19–23.

Chapter 5
Survey: Motivation and Self-regulation

> *I think educational psychology should have two complementary goals for future teachers. The first goal is to teach future teachers to become more effective learners. The second goal is to teach them to be more effective teachers. I believe that attaining the first goal may help in the attainment of the second goal.*
>
> Dembo (2001, p. 25).

Abstract This chapter focuses on the critical roles teacher candidates' self-report of their learning and teaching experiences have in their development as aspiring teachers. Through survey reports, four teacher candidates have an opportunity to demonstrate their readiness for teaching, their perception of the teaching profession, and their self-regulation of learning that is needed for successfully completing their teaching training. The importance of self-regulation of learning during student teaching was found to be an important component in the success of the four teacher candidates. An investigation of all four teacher candidates' cognitive, motivational, and self-regulatory perceptions of their learning and teaching preparation was a significant component of the case study. Self-report questionnaires used to collect data are validated instruments from which mean differences are reported. The purpose of examining these self-reports is not to make generalizations, but to understand the direction and magnitude of these associations. The findings point to the reality that self-regulation of learning in teacher preparation programs has been largely neglected while they are so highly needed among teachers who could teach in diverse and urban communities.

Keyword Self-regulation · Correlation · Assessment · Self-report · Self-regulatory skills · Delay of gratification · Self-efficacy · Help seeking

5.1 Introduction

The four teacher candidates responded to a questionnaire during their student teaching experience. Teacher candidates were situated in an empty classroom to respond to the surveys without time constraints. The surveys contain a collection

© The Author(s) 2015
H. Bembenutty et al., *Developing Self-regulation of Learning and Teaching Skills Among Teacher Candidates*, SpringerBriefs in Education,
DOI 10.1007/978-94-017-9950-8_5

of validated instruments. The purpose of this self-report measure was to examine students' cognitive, motivational, and self-regulatory perception of their learning and teaching preparation from their own perspective. Self-reports have the significant benefits of assisting individuals to externalize in a non-threatening way their experiences and their beliefs. Although questionnaires have the limitation of being sensitive to social desirability and self-representation bias, they can be used as instruments for individuals to project inner thoughts that otherwise they would not be likely to express or share (Pintrich and DeGroot 1990). Although an individual structured interview was conducted with the participants and the survey assessed similar constructs, participants had more flexibility using self-report questionnaires to express their thoughts without being pressured by face-to-face interaction. Additionally, communication skills are much less a factor in the quality of the answers gained using this type of measurement tool.

Obtaining correlational data helps researchers to collect a significant amount of data that they cannot acquire from experimental research. Given that correlational data are gathered outside of a laboratory setting, it resembles everyday life and realistic situations. Consequently, correlational data is considered to be a good starting point for initial investigations and can provide possible directions for future experimental studies. Thus, the interpretation of correlational data can be helpful to research that investigates naturally occurring associations that otherwise may not be practical or ethical to explore. For instance, it would be considered unethical to assign teacher candidates to a control condition that it is not beneficial to their success in the program.

Correlational analyses only show relationships between variables. Thus, cause and effect cannot be determined and we cannot identify which variable is having an effect on the others. In addition, it is too difficult to identify a possible third variable that may be a factor in the relationship of the correlated variables.

The purpose of examining self-reports in this case study is not to make generalizations, but to understand the direction and magnitude of these associations. The design of this case study does not have the strengths of rigorous experimental research because it does not have a control group and independent variables were not manipulated. Correlations are very sensitive to sample size and given our small sample size, our case study is not immune to this problem. Readers are encouraged to consider these points while interpreting the findings of the correlational data in the present case study.

5.2 Instruments

Ohio Teacher Sense of Efficacy Scale. The Teacher Efficacy Scale (OTSES; Short version), a 24-item scale (Tschannen-Moran and Hoy 2001) measures teachers' efficacy of student engagement, instructional strategies, and classroom management. Participants were instructed to indicate their personal opinion about each statement by circling the appropriate response at the right of each statement. The short version used in this study contains 10 items. Sample items were: "If a student did not remember information I gave in a previous lesson, I would know how to increase his/her retention in the next lesson" and "If a student in my class becomes disruptive and noisy, I feel assured that I know some techniques to redirect him/her quickly." The format for all items in the survey was a 6-point scale, ranging from 1(strongly agree) through 6 (strongly disagree). Internal consistency reliability, as estimated by Cronbach alpha, was 0.82 for the present sample ($M = 4.37, SD = 0.85$).

Self-efficacy for Learning Scale. This instrument measured preservice teachers' judgments of confidence about learning the content of the materials for student teaching in which they were enrolled (Bembenutty 2010). Self-efficacy items were worded as follows: "I am sure that I can learn all the material for student teaching." Rating scale options ranged from 1 (strongly disagree) to 7 (strongly agree) ($M = 6.87, SD = 0.56$).

Academic Delay of Gratification Scale. The students responded to the 10 scenarios on the Academic Delay of Gratification Scale (ADOGS; Bembenutty and Karabenick 1998, 2004). The ADOGS examines students' delay of gratification preference in relation to student teaching in which participants were enrolled when they responded to the study. The ADOGS assesses content-specific and course-specific delay of gratification. The students rated their preference for an immediately available attractive option versus a delayed alternative. An example is "Go to a favorite movie and then rush to complete the lesson plan for student teaching" versus "Postpone going to the movies until after you have completed the lesson plans for student teaching." Students responded on a 4-point scale: "Definitely choose A," "Probably choose A," "Probably choose B," and "Definitely choose B." Delay of gratification was considered here as a continuous variable; thus, responses were coded and added for the 10 items, then divided by 10 so that higher total scores indicated greater delay of gratification (range 1–4). Internal consistency reliability, as estimated by Cronbach alpha, was 0.78 ($M = 3.72, SD = 0.37$).

Perceived Responsibility for Learning. It was assessed with an 18-item scale adapted from Kitsantas and Zimmerman (2009). Teacher candidates rated the extent to which they believe that learning is their responsibility or the instructor's responsibility. Magno (2011) and Ramdass and Bembenutty (2012) used Kitsantas and Zimmerman's scale and found associations between perceiving one as primarily responsible and academic performance. An item example is, "Who is more responsible for not finishing music homework assignments?" Students answered using the following seven-point scale: 1 (mainly the teacher), 2 (definitely more the teacher), 3 (slightly more the teacher), 4 (both equally), 5 (slightly more the student), 6 (definitely more the student), and 7 (mainly the student). The Cronbach's alpha was 0.85 ($M = 3.41, SD = 1.34$).

Intrinsic Motivation Scale. Students responded to an instrument which assessed their intrinsic interest in the course and in the material they were learning (Bembenutty 2010). A sample item from the scale was: "I enjoy studying for student teaching more than for other subjects." Rating scale options ranged from 1(strongly disagree) to 7 (strongly agree). Internal consistency reliability, as estimated by Cronbach alpha, was 0.57 ($M = 6.40, SD = 0.56$).

Outcome Expectancy Scale. Students were asked three questions about their beliefs about whether student teaching would have long-term benefits (Bembenutty 2010). An example item is "Student teaching would enhance my future job skills." Responses were based on a Likert Scale with choices ranging from 1 (strongly disagree) to 7 (strongly agree). The reliability coefficient was 0.87 ($M = 7.00$, $SD = 0.00$).

Self-regulation of Learning. To assess the use of self-regulated learning strategies such as goal-setting, lesson planning, self-monitoring, and self-evaluation in the course in which they were currently enrolled, the students responded to an academic self-regulation scale (Bembenutty 2010). A sample item from this scale was: "I keep a record of any completed lesson plans for student teaching." Rating scale options ranged from 1 (strongly disagree) to 7 (strongly agree). Internal consistency reliability, as estimated by Cronbach alpha, was 0.56 ($M = 6.46$, $SD = 0.41$).

Self-regulation of Student Teaching. To assess the use of self-regulated learning strategies such as goal-setting, lesson planning, self-monitoring, and self-evaluation in relation to student teaching in the course in which they were currently enrolled, the students responded to an academic self-regulation scale (Bembenutty 2010). A sample item from this scale was: "How often do you keep a record on how well you are doing in this course in preparation for the final examination?" Rating scale options ranged from 1 (never) to 7 (always). Internal consistency reliability, as estimated by Cronbach alpha, was 0.86 ($M = 6.25$, $SD = 0.66$).

Teacher Candidates' Reported Help Seeking. This scale has four subscales related to seeking help when student teaching tasks are too difficult for the participants to accomplish on their own. Specifically, the scales measure their efforts as teacher candidates when it comes to seeking help regarding student teaching. Although help seeking is a considered a self-regulatory learning strategy, in the current investigation it is operationalized separate from self-regulation to emphasize help seeking's unique contribution to the development of the four teacher candidates. Delineating help seeking as a separate component will highlight the important contribution of help seeking to teachers' self-regulated learning.

- *Adaptive Help Seeking*: Teacher candidates reported their adaptive help seeking from their instructors during student teaching (an example item is, "When I ask for help with assignments pertaining to this class project, I prefer to be given hints or clues rather than the answer," ($M = 6.00$; $SD = 1.45$; $\alpha = 0.77$) and from their peers during student teaching (an example item is "When I ask a peer for help with my work, I don't want my peer to give away the whole answer," ($M = 6.90$; $SD = 0.57$; $\alpha = 0.67$; White 2011).

- *Executive Help Seeking*: Teacher candidates reported executive help-seeking tendencies from their instructors during student teaching (an example item is "When I ask the instructor for help with assignments pertaining to this class project, I prefer the instructor do the work for me rather than explain to me how to do it," $M = 1.20$; $SD = 0.40$; $\alpha = 0.78$) and from their peers during student teaching (an example item is "When I ask a peer for help on tasks

I don't understand pertaining to student teaching, I ask that the student do it for me;" $M = 1.05$; $SD = 1.00$; $\alpha = 0.00$; White 2011).

- *Avoidance Help Seeking*: Teacher candidates reported executive help-seeking tendencies from their instructors during student teaching (an example item is "If I need help with the sections of the tasks pertaining to student teaching, I prefer to skip it rather than to ask for help," $M = 1.41$; $SD = 0.63$; $\alpha = 0.89$; White 2011).
- *Perceived Benefits of Help Seeking*: Teacher candidates reported executive help-seeking tendencies from their instructors during student teaching (an example item is "I like to ask for help about my tasks pertaining student teaching;" $M = 6.64$; $SD = 1.72$; $\alpha = 0.98$; White 2011).

5.3 Correlation Among Variables

Given the limited sample size, correlations can only be considered for their direction and magnitude without considering the critical p-values. In light of that, the results revealed that teacher self-efficacy was positively associated with self-regulation for learning ($r = 0.21$), perceived responsibility ($r = 0.61$), and help-seeking benefits ($r = 0.29$). These findings suggest that teacher candidates who reported high teaching self-efficacy beliefs also reported that they put effort into regulating their learning process during student teaching and that they perceived benefit from seeking help from skilled teachers and peers and believed that the responsibility of students' learning rests primarily on them rather than on the students. However, teacher self-efficacy was negatively related to delay of gratification ($r = -0.36$), adaptive help seeking from instructors ($r = -0.61$) and from peers ($r = -0.72$). These findings suggest that their teacher self-efficacy was not yet fully integrated into their teacher schemata with regard to the importance of delaying gratification and seeking help. These discrepancies are understandable given that maturing as teachers is a developmental process that requires time and continuous nurturing. On the other hand, these findings are consistent with what was observed among the teacher candidates in that they did engage in a significant effort to delay gratification and help seek while their teacher self-efficacy was developing.

Academic delay of gratification was correlated with self-efficacy for learning ($r = 0.84$), intrinsic interest ($r = 0.99$), self-regulation for learning ($r = 0.76$) and for student teaching ($r = 0.86$), help-seeking benefits ($r = 0.45$), and perceived responsibility ($r = 0.41$). These findings suggest that teacher candidates who were willing to postpone immediate, attractive activities (e.g., going to a party) were also those who enjoyed learning, and self-regulated their learning and student teaching processes while appreciating the benefits of seeking help and considered themselves highly responsibility for their students' learning and academic performance. However, there is an inverse relation between delay of gratification and adaptive help seeking from instructors ($r = -0.21$) and avoidance help seeking ($r = -0.29$).

In general, teacher candidates reported use of help-seeking strategies tended to be negatively related to their reported motivational and other self-regulatory processes. For instance, adaptive help seeking from instructors was negatively correlated to self-regulation ($r = -0.79$). These findings are obviously inconsistent with their observed behaviors. A conclusion drawn from their own observations finds that these students tended to have developed appropriate help-seeking skills during their teaching preparation training.

5.4 Mean Differences Among Teacher Candidates

The four teacher candidates reported similar patterns of beliefs, motivation, and behavior (see Table 5.1). With regard to teacher self-efficacy beliefs, Chris and Jaime reported lower beliefs than Maria and Angela. With regard to academic delay of gratification, Angela reported the lowest willingness to delay gratification during student teaching, but she did not differ from the other three teacher candidates in relation to self-efficacy for learning. All four teacher candidates reported consistent self-efficacy beliefs and outcome expectancy. Chris and Angela reported lower self-regulation for learning than Maria and Jaime, but Jaime and Angela reported the lowest self-regulation of student teaching.

With regard to the use of help-seeking strategies, Maria and Jaime reported the lowest adaptive help-seeking strategies from instructors and the lowest adaptive help seeking from peers. Chris reported the highest adaptive help-seeking strategies from both the instructor and the peers. While Jaime reported the highest

Table 5.1 Mean and standard deviation for variables in the survey

Variable	Chris	Maria	Jaime	Angela	Group mean	Standard deviation
Teacher's self-efficacy	3.50	5.20	3.80	5.00	4.37	0.85
Academic delay of gratification	4.00	4.00	3.70	3.20	3.72	0.37
Self-efficacy for learning	7.00	7.00	6.75	6.75	6.87	0.56
Intrinsic motivation	6.80	6.80	6.40	5.60	6.40	0.56
Outcome expectancy	7.00	7.00	7.00	7.00	7.00	0.00
Self-regulation of learning	6.36	7.00	6.50	6.00	6.46	0.41
Self-regulation of student teaching	6.73	6.91	5.73	5.64	6.25	0.66
Perceived responsibility	3.50	5.11	1.83	3.22	3.41	1.34
Adaptive help seeking (instructors)	7.60	4.20	5.60	6.60	6.00	1.45
Adaptive help seeking (peers)	7.60	6.20	6.80	7.00	6.90	0.57
Executive help seeking (instructors)	1.00	1.00	1.80	1.00	1.20	0.40
Executive help seeking (peers)	1.00	1.00	1.20	1.00	1.05	1.00
Avoidance help seeking	1.00	1.00	2.33	1.33	1.41	0.63
Benefits of help seeking	7.86	8.00	4.29	6.43	6.64	1.72

executive help-seeking tendencies, the other three teacher candidates reported lower than Jaime, which suggests that Chris, Maria, and Angela tend to seek help more frequently for mastering tasks than for just getting the work done for them.

Jaime and Angela reported higher tendencies to engage in avoidance help-seeking behavior than Chris and Maria. Jaime and Angela also reported the lower help-seeking benefits while Chris and Maria reported getting the highest benefits from help seeking in general. In relation to perceived responsibility for learning, Maria reported that the student is slightly more responsible for learning than the teacher is while Jaime reported that the teacher is definitely more responsible than the student. Chris and Angela reported that the teacher is only slightly more responsible than the student.

5.5 Putting It Together

Self-regulation of learning during student teaching has been revealed as an important component associated with the academic success of the four teacher candidates. These findings point to the reality that self-regulation of learning in teacher preparation programs has been largely neglected (Goetz et al. 2013). In addition, the findings revealed that teacher preparation programs should pay closer attention to the different self-regulatory competencies that are known to be associated with academic success. Teacher candidates need to learn self-regulation in order to be able to plan and implement instruction, assess students learning, and reflect upon instructional and assessment outcomes.

Teacher self-efficacy is also associated with teacher retention, motivation, job satisfaction, positive relation with administration, and low level of stress and burnout. Teacher candidates need to enhance their teacher self-efficacy beliefs since the association between teacher self-efficacy beliefs and multiple teaching outcomes, such as students' motivation, homework, classroom management, and positive relation with parents is well established in the literature.

Training teacher candidates to appreciate the myriad of benefits of delaying gratification is an important outcome derived from these four teacher candidates' reports. For instance, teacher candidates who understand the value of postponing immediately available but low valuable tasks would be the ones who would create interesting lesson plans with solid and accurate content and with attention to diverse learners.

Help seeking is an essential self-regulatory strategy that these four teacher candidates reported with mixed and conflicting tendencies. For instance, adaptive help seeking was negatively related to self-regulation for learning ($r = -0.79$), when from other research with teacher candidates, we found a positive association (White and Bembenutty 2013). Effective teaching preparation programs need to include effective training on self-regulation among teacher candidates.

References

Bembenutty, H. (2010). Homework completion: The role of self-efficacy, delay of gratifica-
tion, and self-regulatory processes. *International Journal of Educational & Psychological
Assessment, 6*(1), 1–20.
Bembenutty, H., & Karabenick, S. A. (1998). Academic delay of gratification. *Learning and
Individual Differences, 10*, 329–346. doi:10.1016/S1041-6080(99)80126-5.
Bembenutty, H., & Karabenick, S. A. (2004). Inherent association between academic delay of
gratification, future time perspective, and self-regulated learning. *Educational Psychology
Review, 16*(1), 35–57. doi:10.1023/B:EDPR.0000012344.34008.5c.
Dembo, M. H. (2001). Learning to teach is not enough: Future teachers also need to learn how to
learn. *Teacher Education Quarterly, 28*(4), 23–35.
Goetz, T., Nett, U. E., & Hall, N. C. (2013). Self-regulated learning. In N. C. Hall & T. Goetz (Eds.),
Emotion, motivation, and self-regulation: A handbook for teachers. Emerald: Bingley, UK.
Kitsantas, A., & Zimmerman, B. J. (2009). College students homework and academic achieve-
ment: The mediating role of self-regulatory beliefs. *Metacognition and Learning, 4*(2),
1556–1623.
Magno, C. (2011). Establishing a scale that measures responsibility for learning. *The International
Journal of Educational and Psychological Assessment, 8*(2), 31–42.
Pintrich, P. R., & De Groot, E. V. (1990). Motivational and self-regulated learning components of
classroom academic performance. *Journal of Educational Psychology, 82*(1), 33–40.
Ramdas, D., & Bembenutty, H. (2012). Exploring self-regulatory behaviors during music prac-
tice among south asian indian american instrumental students. *The International Journal of
Research and Review, 9*, 1–31.
Tschannen-Moran, M., & Hoy, A. W. (2001). Teacher efficacy: Capturing an elusive construct.
Teaching and teacher education, 17(7), 783–805.
White, M. C. (2011). Predicting success in teacher certification testing: The role of academic
help seeking. *International Journal of Educational and Psychological Assessment, 7*(1),
24–44.
White, M. C., & Bembenutty, H. (2013). Not all avoidance help seekers are created equal
individual differences in adaptive and executive help seeking. *SAGE Open, 3*(2), 1–14.
doi:10.1177/2158244013484916.

Chapter 6
Student Teaching Interview

> *While academic deficits are often addressed through remedial programs and workshops, teacher education programs would benefit from early awareness of self-regulatory behaviors evidenced by incoming students. Exploration of these areas of development, linkage to constructs prominent in the study of self-regulation, academic motivation, and strategy use can help teacher educators determine the degree to which specific areas of development impact success in teacher education programs for individual students.*
>
> White and Bembenutty (2013, p. 2).

Abstract This chapter examines four teacher candidates' perception of their teaching readiness by providing them a forum during a structured-interview where they could be free to share their reflection of who they are and how they perceived their aspiring profession. The interviews were conducted in person with three instructors while they were student teaching and in writing after completing their teaching training. Self-reflective practice among teacher candidates gives them an opportunity to externalize inner thoughts, feeling, and beliefs. Through the interviews, it was learned the four teacher candidates' perception of learners, their degree of self-efficacy beliefs, how they use self-regulatory strategies, their perception of diverse and urban learners, classroom management skills, willingness to delay gratification, and perception of the support they have received by their institution, faculty, and peers. The interviews revealed that help seeking was for these four teachers a paramount self-regulatory strategy, which they attributed to the success of their teaching training.

Keywords Structured-interview · Teacher candidates · Self-regulation · Delay of gratification · Culture · Self-efficacy · Classroom management

The four teacher candidates were invited to participate individually in a structured interview conducted by three educators with whom they were familiar (see Appendix E). The purpose of the interview was to assess the teacher candidates' perception of their teaching training experience. The interviews were conducted

© The Author(s) 2015
H. Bembenutty et al., *Developing Self-regulation of Learning and Teaching Skills Among Teacher Candidates*, SpringerBriefs in Education,
DOI 10.1007/978-94-017-9950-8_6

in a familiar and unthreatening environment. Two of the interviewers were the teacher candidate's college professors and the third interviewer had a long-term professional relationship with the teacher candidates. The interviews took place in the School of Education's computer and study laboratory.

The three researchers who conducted the interviews developed the questions and reached 100 % agreement about the interview's content validity and reliability. Nine questions were constructed, and each interviewer was assigned to ask three specific questions during the interview. Each of the interviewers took written notes during the interview and rated the quality of the answers provided by the students. Each question had follow up questions to be used when the teacher candidates needed to elaborate their answers. In order to provide a clear and comprehensive analysis of the information gathered from the interviews, we provide examples of the students responses followed by a critical analysis and synthesis of the major themes derived from the interview (Zimmerman and Pons 1986).

6.1 Interview Questions and Example Answers

1. *How do you perceive your students? Can all of the students learn? What are the students' responsibilities in the classroom? What are your responsibilities in their learning?*

Chris responded:

> When I have had disruptive students, I have been able to intervene one to one and fol-
> low up with informal talks. I often look at student's body language first to see if there
> is a behavior problem about to occur. That is when I sit with the student to prevent an
> outburst, and I intervene before anything happens. This is how I build relationships with
> disruptive students, and I see it as one of my most important roles in the classroom. When
> I am teaching, I use post it notes to remind students of their strengths. Phrases such as:
> "You are smart!" "You have strengths!" "You are learning!" always build confidence.

> I must keep learning so I can be a better teacher to the students that "don't
> get it." The teacher is more responsible than the students because she has
> more knowledge and can work with each student until them "get it."

Angela responded:

> I see all my students as wonderful. They challenge me to improve my teaching, I learn
> from them. I believe all students can learn but they have different educational needs and
> grasp information differently. I closely observe how each student is processing while I am
> teaching and look for moments when they might need help. I must keep learning so I can
> be a better teacher to the students that "don't get it." The teacher is more responsible than
> the students because she has more knowledge and can work with each student until they

"get it." When working one to one with a student who "does not get it," it is important for the teacher to let the student ask questions and then together find the answers. Both the teacher and the student have to share responsibility. In order for the student to learn the teacher has to teach him how to learn.

2. How confident are you that you can teach your students? Can you motivate all learners? Do you have all the necessary skills to help all your students?

Maria responded:

> I have most of the skills that I need to teach in general (youth group), but I still need to ask the cooperating teacher and my professor for help to teach in the classroom. There are some things I need to relearn. I can motivate my students to learn by having them start somewhere. I find out what they can do and ask them to begin by doing something they can do, like drawing rather than writing a sentence. I have to remember that they want to learn but they have different ways of learning. I need to find out what they can do. I have skills; I just need to get more experience.

Jaime responded:

> Sometimes, I am nervous because of my age, but I am still confident that I can teach. I have been told that I have teacher presence. I want my students to learn, and I tell them that in the end it is the student that does the work, but I can play a big role by teaching them what they need to do to learn. It is my responsibility to motivate the students. Sometimes in the moment when I am not sure if it is going well, I still know that I can teach and motivate my students to learn.

3. Are you a self-regulated student?

Jaime responded:

> Somewhat. I notice things that are happening while I am teaching, and then I change the direction of lesson plan to make corrections. I feel very strongly that I have the skills to complete the lesson even when I am nervous. Feedback (post it notes) from the teacher helped me make changes to the way I was doing the lesson. When I feel nervous, I want to just keep going on with the lesson, but now I am better at self-monitoring during my teaching.

Chris responded:

> I engage in time management, I had to make decisions about spending time with friends or getting my lesson plans done. My attitude in the classroom is positive. I push myself to be positive so the students can have a positive learning environment. I am organized, and it helps me to stay on track to see if what I am doing is working. I remind myself of specific things I need to do with individual students by using post-its and placing them on desks or chairs as reminders. I establish new goals for myself and for my students. By sharing my goals with them it helps them to grow. I use post-test assessments to re-evaluate my whole lesson. I ask the teacher if I did what I set out to do, and what can I change? I use the feedback to make changes. I am not only looking for positive feedback but for what I can add to the lesson to see a better outcome.

4. Please tell us about your efforts to seek help when a lesson plan or a class does not go well (e.g., when the students misbehave, to get information for your lesson, when you do not understand something, when the tasks are too difficult for you to accomplish on your own, by whom, to learn or to get answers).

Chris responded:

> I send e-mails to the cooperating teacher before I present a lesson asking her what I could do better and for feedback. During the lesson, I modify it if it is necessary. If the children had trouble with the lesson, I ask the teacher for help, and it helps me to plan the next lesson. I use visuals and auditory tools. I also ask the college supervisor, other teachers, and peers. I prefer to seek help from the cooperating teacher but the math coach has also been helpful in sharing his expertise. At times, I ask for help from the cooperating teacher while I am teaching so I can modify "on the spot".

Maria responded:

> I definitely seek help from everyone! The teachers, my peers, my cooperating teacher, and the reading specialist are some of the people I ask for help. I ask my cooperating teacher for advice on how to keep the attention of the student while I am teaching. I spend time observing the reading teacher to learn more about literacy. I use the Internet for research, read, and use many textbooks to learn more about the subjects I am teaching.

5. *Can you help your students to be self-regulated learners? How? Give examples*

Jaime responded:

> I like to have my students helping each other. My goals are the same for all of them because I think all students need to be on the "same page." I focus on drills.

Maria responded:

> Absolutely! I help them to set goals to be better and to be accountable for their own behavior. I have my students keeping journals. I create group work so they can learn from each other. I set goals together with the students for classroom management. I create individual goals and have weekly interviews to keep up goals.

6. *Can you help your students to delay gratification for the sake of learning? How? Give examples*

Jaime responded:

> All students struggle with delay of gratification. I see delay of gratification as discipline. I make sure they are aware of the consequences of their behavior if they choose to go to a party before doing their work.

Chris responded:

> I help students with delay of gratification to a certain degree. I model delay of gratification by showing them how to wait. I help the students by being available after school or during lunch hours or preparation hours. I clarify the importance of putting things off to look to the future. Parental influence comes into play with regard to delay of gratification. I schedule meetings with parents to show them their children's grades so they can see the bigger picture. I try to help them attribute low grades with time spent playing video games and ask the parents to participate in making the plan.

7. *What is your philosophy of teaching? Why? Tell us about your classroom management beliefs. What are some of the classroom management strategies that you use in your classroom?*

Chris responded:

> I believe that all children can learn and that they learn differently. I believe that the teacher creates the environment. I believe that we learn from our students. With regard to classroom management, everything needs to be organized, and there needs to be respect between student-student and student-teacher. Parents are active members of the classroom. I reach out to every parent and let him or her know I am approachable. I teach parents how to seek help. Parents' involvement is beneficial.

Angela responded:

> We are to be role models and go beyond what is expected of us. I was independent but I learned it was alright to seek help. I believe all kids can learn in a safe environment. I do not want to embarrass them and as a role model I need to create trust. My role is to guide them. Parents are part of the class.

8. *Tell us about how you perceive or expect to help students from diverse backgrounds (e.g., ethnicity, gender, cognitive or physical disability, language, and exceptionality)?*

Jaime responded:

> I believe in creating a loving, accepting, not judgmental environment where all students feel included by the teacher and with each other. I need to create lessons that make each student feel welcome. I need to learn the characteristics that make up their culture and what their comfort levels are when asked to share. To promote gender equality and respect for each other I teach manners and mix genders. I have mixed seating arrangements so students can help each other. I promote differentiated instruction to challenge them and meet with students 1:1 to help them.

> I believe that all children can learn and that they learn differently. I believe that the teacher creates the environment. I believe that we learn from our students.

Maria responded:

> I need to learn about each individual culture from many perspectives and incorporate it into the classroom (e.g., music, art). I need to learn about culture, language, and environments. As far as gender, we are all equal. I plan lessons to include all students, different and individualized. For ELL students I think they should master their first language while working on their second. I provide translated curriculum for these students. I challenge my gifted students by bringing it up a notch and adding higher order thinking questions.

9. *How has the college's educational program influenced your teaching practice and your philosophy of classroom management? (If you are not teaching, answer the question in relation to your current education.)*

Jaime responded:

> This is a college where students are shown love and encouraged to have faith; it helped me
> to have faith. I was not only encouraged to be a teacher, but in my academics too. I know
> that in this college, I am not alone. I have support here with people who care about me.

Chris responded:

> The college creates a safe atmosphere. I learned about self-efficacy. The college opened
> doors for me as a learner and an individual. I was both stretched and sheltered. The col-
> lege had high expectations for my learning and helped me set goals that seemed impossi-
> ble, yet we accomplished them, and I am empowered. Here we have a family and our faith
> unites us and makes the experience amazing.

6.2 What Have We Found So Far?

As is indicated by the responses from these four teacher candidates, their teacher
training experiences contain many similarities. However, the four teacher candidates are not identical. Their responses were rated differently by the three instructors (see Table 6.1). Out of the four teacher candidates, most of Jaime's responses
received the lowest ratings while most of Chris's responses received the highest
ratings.

Although there are differences among their answers, there are some common themes that emerged from the conversational interview conducted with the
students.

- *Perception of their students*: All of the four teacher candidates reported that they
  believe that all learners can learn. They expressed that the teacher is responsible
  for the learning of the students. They also believe that all the students are equal
  but can learn in different ways.
- *Differentiated instruction*: The four teacher candidates expressed that differentiated instruction is important for effective learning. They believe that differentiated instruction could help them to teach all learners while providing attention
  to their individual needs.
- *Culture*: These four teacher candidates strongly believe that any instruction and
  interaction with their students' needs to be channeled through the cultural differences of the students. By culture, they referred to ethnicity, gender, cognitive
  or physical disability, language, and exceptionality. They are convinced that it is
  their responsibility to consider and assimilate these cultural factors into instructional planning, choice of vocabulary and teaching students.
- *Self-efficacy beliefs*: From statements made during the interviews, it is clearly
  observed that these teacher candidates possessed an acceptable level of self-
  efficacy—both, self-efficacy about learning and teacher's self-efficacy. They
  believe that they have the skills and disposition to learn and the training to be
  good teachers.

Table 6.1   Faculty rating of the quality of answers by teacher candidates

Question	Raters	Teacher candidates			
		Jaime	Maria	Chris	Angela
1. How do you perceive your students?	Rater 1	3	6	7	7
	Rater 2	6	6	7	7
	Rater 3	4	6	7	7
2. How confident are you that you can teach your students	Rater 1	4	6	7	7
	Rater 2	4	6	7	6
	Rater 3	5	7	6	6
3. Are you a self-regulated teacher candidate?	Rater 1	3	5	7	6
	Rater 2	2	7	7	6
	Rater 3	3	6	7	6
4. Please tell us about your efforts to seek help when a lesson plan or a class does not go well?	Rater 1	3	7	7	6
	Rater 2	5	7	7	6
	Rater 3	2	7	7	6
5. Can you help your students to be self-regulated learners?	Rater 1	2	6	4	3
	Rater 2	2	7	5	1
	Rater 3	2	7	5	2
6. Can you help your students to delay gratification for the sake of learning?	Rater 1	2	4	5	6
	Rater 2	2	4	5	2
	Rater 3	2	4	5	2
7. What is your philosophy of teaching?	Rater 1	4	5	7	7
	Rater 2	4	6	7	6
	Rater 3	5	7	7	5
8. Tell us about how you perceive or expect to help students from diverse backgrounds	Rater 1	5	7	7	7
	Rater 2	6	7	7	7
	Rater 3	6	6	6	7
9. How has the college's educational program influenced your teaching practice and your philosophy of classroom management?	Rater 1	4	7	7	7
	Rater 2	6	7	7	7
	Rater 3	6	6	7	7

- *Perception of the college*: These four teacher candidates reported that attending a college with high academic standards challenged them to be better students. They spoke very highly about the staff and instructors of the college. Choosing to attend a faith based college also added to their spiritual development and strengthened their faith.
- *Classroom management*: All four teacher candidates clearly stated that classroom management is a significant challenge. However, they also knew how to seek help from knowledgeable people when they needed it.
- *Help seeking*: At the end of the teaching training, these four teacher candidates were knowledgeable about the theory of help seeking and very often employed those strategies when they encountered challenges. Help seeking is clearly embedded in their teaching practice.

- *Self-regulation*: Self-regulation was a challenge for these four teacher candidates, but they reported that they are learning how to set goals, engage in self-monitoring, seek help when it is needed, and sustain motivation. They practice self-reflection and self-evaluation.
- *Academic delay of gratification*: The teacher candidates recognized the challenges of delaying gratification but they reported that they help their students by making them aware of the consequences of their behaviors and by setting goals. From their interviews, it is clear that this is an area in which they need more training.
- *Parents*: These teacher candidates strongly believe that parents are very important team members for the benefit of students' learning. They report that they welcome parents into their classrooms and value what they contribute. All four teacher candidates expressed their desire to work with parents and the community to improve student achievement.

> The teacher candidates recognized the challenges of delaying gratification but they reported that they help their students by making them aware of the consequences of their behaviors and by setting goals. From their interviews, it is clear that this is an area in which they need more training.

6.3 Post-graduation Interview

A year after completing their educational training and graduating from college, the four students were sent by e-mail a questionnaire (see Appendix F). They were invited to reflect about their current professional status, their motivation, self-regulation, and help- seeking skills. They were invited to share their thoughts, experiences, and beliefs related to their academic and student teaching experiences. They were instructed that there were no right or wrong answers and that they could respond to all the questions or only to those they were comfortable answering. They were instructed that their answer would not affect their job or academic status or their relationship with the current or former educators. The instructions indicate that there was not financial compensation for their participation.

At that point, three of them had obtained their teacher certification but another did not attempt to retake the Content Specialty Test (CST) after an initial failing score of only a few points. This particular student moved out of the state which required all teacher certification exams be retaken (PRAXIS) and while preparing for the new exams enrolled in an education master's programs and tutored children. She then became employed by a legal firm and was promoted into the position of a legal assistant and translator where she utilizes the skills she learned in college to help the law firm teach non-English speaking clients about the criminal justice legal system.

Below, we included representative answers to the questions included in the post-graduation questionnaire followed by an analysis and synthesis of the answers provided by the students.

6.4 Examples of Responses to the Post-graduation Questionnaire

1. *How do you perceive your students? Can all of the students learn? What are the students' responsibilities in the classroom? What are your responsibilities in their learning?*

Jaime responded:

> I see my students as very capable and intelligent young boys and girls who have great potential. I only look at their weaknesses as an opportunity for their strengths to shine through. I believe that all of my students are able to learn. Every child is different, and I find any possible way to help them overcome their weaknesses by being the best teacher that I can be to them. Five important things that I feel I need as a teacher are love, patience, passion, knowledge, and discipline. I need to make sure I have all the resources I need. If I am lacking in any necessities, I need to do whatever it takes to get them so that it can help the students' learning. I will not be able to accomplish this task if I do not have any passion motivating me to do so. I need to have lots of patience when my students are not getting the material and are getting frustrated at improving. I also need to make sure I show them love and discipline. I had a similar situation with a kindergartner. One of my students was not doing well in school and I could see the frustration in his eyes. However, I did not let this frustrate me as well because they could sense it if I did. I used every resource I could, was knowledgeable in everything I needed to know, and continued working with him day by day patiently. With the help of his family and myself, he improved drastically! The students' responsibility is to be attentive, respectful, adhere to instructions, be obedient, be willing to learn, believe in themselves, and have fun. If the student follows these simple responsibilities, they will be able to succeed in school with the help of the teacher and family.

Angela responded:

> I don't know exactly how I perceive my students. There are so many words to describe them, but one thing I learned from tutoring is that they like attention. And the more attention they are given (and talked to like adults), the more they get into the lessons and are able to pay more attention. I believe that all students can learn at their own pace. While tutoring students from first to 8th grade this past year, I noticed that they all take time to learn a lesson, and while others can learn it right away, they can also forget about it in months. Yet when they learn it at their pace, it can stay with them or at least, they are able to remember it. I believe the student's responsibilities in the classroom are to maintain the classroom's organization, to learn, to talk, and to ask for help. My responsibility is to ensure that they learn, that they are able to grasp the lesson, and when asked, they will be able to show and tell me they have understood. My responsibility is to do all that is possible for them to succeed even if it means asking for help myself.

2. How confident are you that you can teach your students? Can you motivate all learners? Do you have all the necessary skills to help all your students?

Maria responded:

I am very confident that I can teach students. I have received an adequate amount of training in the teaching field and have had the opportunity to substitute in very low functioning schools and have seen what is waiting for me out there. However, because I am not a fulltime teacher yet, I feel as though I still need that experience to become very highly confident in teaching. I believe I can motivate all learners. I think a way to do so is to really get to know the students individually. Knowing what their interests are and understanding their functioning level is a benefit in motivating all learners. I believe I have the necessary skills to help all my students. The first skill is to know that they have the ability to learn. The second skill is that I am a great communicator. I think staying in communication with the student, family members, professionals, and other people that are involved in the students' life is a critical skill needed to help the student learn to the their highest ability. My role in my students' learning experience is to be an effective teacher. If I do not have a positive effect on my students' learning experience, then there is no point in teaching. A big portion is dependent on me for their leaning and academic achievement. It is my duty to provide high support in order to anticipate high expectations from my students.

Jaime responded:

In the beginning of my student teaching, my confidence was very low. It was not until I began teaching in my own classroom that my confidence increased tremendously. I am very confident in knowing that I can teach my students. I can definitely motivate my learners. I believe I have all the necessary skills to help my students depending on what kinds of students I have. For example, since I am a perfectionist, I need to make sure I am knowledgeable in every aspect of cerebral palsy before I begin to teach a child that has cerebral palsy. In my current classroom that I am teaching, however, I have every skill that I need to help all of my students. If I were placed in a classroom filled with students of disabilities, I would need to make sure I have all the resources I need as well as the knowledge. I believe that my role is very important when it comes to the students' learning experience. I need to make sure I have created a positive and healthy environment within the classroom as well as having a good routine and teaching style for my students. I personally feel that a big part of my teaching will influence his or her learning and academic achievement.

> I am very confident in helping my students become self-regulated learners. I make sure to give them enough guidance along the way so that one day they can fulfill the task all by themselves.

3. Are you a self-regulated student?

Jaime responded:

I believe that I am very highly self-regulated as a teacher because I take full control of and evaluate my own learning and behavior in the classroom. I am very much aware of my learning styles and make sure to monitor my teaching as well as the students' learning. My time management has improved tremendously. I would not have gotten better at my time management if I did not continue monitoring myself and worked through trial and error. I have also improved greatly in partnering with other teachers and parents to help the student as well as my teaching.

Chris responded:

I believe that most of the time I am a self-regulated teacher. This year alone I was faced with the challenge of not having the proper resources needed for my students. I went to Barnes and Noble and bought several teaching resources and was able to produce and execute lessons that were successful.

4. *Please tell us about your efforts to seek help when a lesson plan or a class do not go well (e.g., when the students misbehave, to get information for your lesson, when you do not understand something, when the tasks are too difficult for you to accomplish on your own, by whom, to learn or to get answers).*

Jaime responded:

I believe that my help seeking has increased tremendously since I began teaching. I realized that I had lots of questions that needed answers. Throughout my teaching experience, I have asked help from other teachers, parents, peers, friends, and family and have received more knowledge than I did before I ever asked. It is always healthy to hear another opinion besides your own, and it has always been an advantage on my part.

Chris responded:

I am fortunate enough to work at a school where there are two lead teachers whose main job is to provide support to teachers. Whenever I did not know/understand how to implement certain principles, I always went to them. I found that after speaking to them, the "seasoned" teachers, I had a better understanding of what was expected of me, and I felt confident in what I was doing.

5. *Can you help your students to be self-regulated learners? How? Give examples*

Jaime responded:

I am very confident in helping my students become self-regulated learners. I make sure to give them enough guidance along the way so that one day they can fulfill the task all by themselves. For example, when one of my students kept asking for my help in reading certain words and sounding it out, I decided to continue guiding and teaching him until I felt he was ready to read and sound out the words on his own. Once I felt I had left him with the right confidence, I left him to do the work on his own, and I didn't check his work until the very end. He would look at me every now and again and tell me he couldn't do a problem or it was too hard for him, but I kept telling him he could do it. Before I knew it, he was able to do it on his own without my help! I also make sure to give my students duties of a monitor in the classroom to help them develop independence, self-regulation, and responsibility.

Maria responded:

I most certainly can help my future students become self-regulated learners. I think the first aspect to teach them is to learn responsibility and respect. I think once they have an understanding that they are responsible for their life actions and that they shall treat themselves, others, and schoolwork with respect they will master the area of accountability. An example of this would be to delay gratification. Students will not be rewarded until they can learn to complete work efficiently and respect others around them.

6. Can you help your students to delay gratification for the sake of learning? How? Give examples

Jaime responded:

> I am well able to help my students delay gratification for the sake of learning. Although my students normally have natural tendencies to want the easy way out in learning, I make sure to challenge them and reward them when I see they are trying their best. The children see this and they are motivated by these rewards. Afterwards, I give out the rewards less often so that the children can be able to do the work given without a reward on their mind, but rather just to do well in school. For example, I would give out random stickers to students who I see are improving or trying their best. Through this, I have seen a handful of students begin to really enjoy that subject to their surprise. For example, one of my students enjoys writing, but I had to continue pushing him and rewarding him when I saw fit, and sooner or later, he would do it on his own without me asking him to. I also make sure to have playtime at the end of the day so that my students are not fixed on playing, but on learning. Even throughout the day while the students are working, if I see they were very attentive and focused on schoolwork, I give them free time or rewards. I have trained my children to think that work comes first, then play.

Chris responded:

> To encourage my students to delay gratification, I set up incentives for the day as well as to work towards to the end of the week. Every morning I have a meeting with my students to discuss how the day will go and what lessons and materials must be covered and completed. I also let them know that once our goals have been met, they will earn tickets, free time, or play a class game at the end of the day. This type of motivation works well with the age group with which I work.

7. What is your philosophy of teaching? Why? Tell us about your classroom management beliefs. What are some of the classroom management strategies that you use in your classroom?

Chris responded:

> My philosophy of teaching is that anyone can learn. In order for that to take place, there must be clear classroom management strategies. The philosophy of the school is that "if I cannot teach, then you cannot learn;" therefore they have a zero tolerance level of problematic students. However, in my classroom I use several strategies to control my classroom. I use a traffic light (red, yellow, and green) poster, where everyone begins on green and if they mess up once their name is moved to yellow. If the child continues to disobey, I then move their name to red. Depending on the situation there is a different consequence. Some of the consequences are a phone call home, loss of recess, no trip, or no free time on Fridays. I also have a ticket system where students receive tickets for good behavior, completed homework packets, being a good citizen, and doing a good deed. The students like the ticket system because at the end of the month they are able to trade them in for prizes.

Angela responded:

> I believe my philosophy of teaching has changed somewhat. I still believe that all children can learn and thrive in a learning environment that is stimulating, comforting, and appropriate to children's abilities. Organization and routine are important in the classroom.

8. *Tell us about how you perceive or expect to help students from diverse backgrounds (e.g., ethnicity, gender, cognitive or physical disability, language, and exceptionality)?*

Jaime responded:

> I gladly welcome every student that enters my classroom. I make sure to understand whatever race, gender, religion, language, exceptionality, or disability. I also make sure to do any necessary research on their condition, so that I can help them to the best of my ability. I want to make sure I am knowledgeable and have the proper resources that I need to take care of my students in a way that will help their learning. For example, I was very understanding of one of my students who had a speech impediment and had occupational therapy. As time passed by, I realized I needed to minimize the amount of sentences he wrote for writing because he never was able to finish all five sentences in time. It was not because of laziness or distraction; it was because his hands would hurt and it was too much of an overload for him. I would also modify the home works and sometimes classwork for him when it was needed. I found it to be very helpful for him because I was working at his pace; not my own. As time progressed, I began seeing him improve and I kept on challenging him until finally he was able to do the work that the entire class was doing. With that said, I am very mindful of every child and their needs and try my very best to have them fulfill their highest potential at whatever level they are at. Teaching is not about me; it is about the child.

Maria responded:

> I expect to help my students from diverse backgrounds to my fullest potential. Educating myself about their background is critical in the sense that it would help me assist them accordingly. The beauty of helping students from different backgrounds is that I have an opportunity to learn about different exceptionalities, ethnicities, disabilities, languages, etc. and see them surpass any boundaries.

9. *How has the college's educational program influenced your teaching practice and your philosophy of classroom management? (If you are not teaching, answer the question in relation to your current education.)*

Jaime responded:

> The School of Education has helped me tremendously in my teaching practices and philosophy of classroom management. Most of my learning in teaching and classroom management really started from my student teaching. Once I began teaching in my own classroom, everything I had learned in school and in student teaching came into play. Once I was able to apply what I'd learned in both, I was able to manage my classroom very well. Although I am learning something new each day, I have acquired much knowledge and feedback on my teaching through this college.

Chris responded:

> Having been a student of the undergraduate teacher education program, I feel that the things I learned in several courses and from observing the professors, I have implemented in my class. The compassion and commitment to students' progress is something the professors demonstrated throughout my entire time in the program. Working with 2nd graders, one must be very patient and understanding that you must repeat directions on a consistent basis. This is part of my classroom management.

6.5 Putting It Together

Responses to the interview's key questions posed to the four teacher candidates were consistent, reflecting general agreement. The quantitative and qualitative differences amongst their replies can be attributed to variations in the depth of their answers. Their perceptions, educational experiences, beliefs, and academic successes in the program are factors in determining the differentiation in their responses.

Among the four teacher candidates, Jaime indicated high levels of self-reflection and self-analysis. Jaime reports that she perceives her students as capable and intelligent individuals that have great potential. She views knowing about students' weaknesses as a teacher's opportunity to focus on the learner's strengths. From a similar perspective, Chris believes that all students can learn; however, recognizing the speed at which this occurs varies from learner to learner. It is the teacher's responsibility to use multiple instructional methods and strategies to help the students meet these benchmarks. The four teacher candidates believe they have the skills required to actually teach their students. These perceptions are supported by their reported high levels of teacher self-efficacy beliefs. For instance, Maria asserted that she is highly confident that she can teach all students and that the teaching training she has received is more than adequate to meet the demands of the profession.

All four teacher candidates shared that they considered themselves to be self-regulated learners who consistently deal with challenges and obstacles to time management. Although they have difficulty scheduling blocks of time for doing academic work they report the ability to get their work done. They report that they engage in self-control of their learning and behavior and consistently self-evaluate their own learning and behavior. When asked about their efforts to seek help when a lesson plan or other class-related activities do not go well, they report that their help-seeking tendencies have improved tremendously during their teaching training. They consider themselves to be help seekers. They use resources effectively and seek help from instructors, cooperating teachers, and peers when needed.

With regard to whether the teacher candidates believe that they help their students to be self-regulated learners, they reported that they believe that they can. Based on their individual experiences and what they have observed, all four teacher candidates share the belief that to promote self-regulation they first need to promote responsibility, accountability, and respect. As teachers, their role is to provide guidance and promote self-confidence in their students. They concur that they are able to help their students to delay gratification for the sake of learning. In addition, as teachers who model self-regulation they will instill self-discipline, persistence, self-evaluation, and a sense of responsibility.

The four teacher candidates are in agreement that their philosophy of teaching has changed during the course of their teacher training. They believe that all children can learn and thrive in a well designed learning environment. Chris stated, "My philosophy of teaching is based on the belief that anyone can learn." Jaime stated, "I strongly believe that teachers can help students reach their fullest potentials." They also indicated that over time their self-efficacy for classroom management has improved significantly.

In accordance with the core values of the college, the teacher candidates embrace working with a diverse community of learners. Responses from all four teacher candidates indicated that they welcome diverse learners in their classrooms. Jaime reported, "I make sure to learn as much as I can about each student's background so I can understand influences of whatever race, gender, religion, language, exceptionality, or disability is represented in my classroom." The four teacher candidates are representative of how the college educates celebrates the contributions from diverse populations. They take pride in the education they received and the investment made by their institution into their futures. Angela related that her time at the institution has benefitted her in many ways. She states being a part of a academically excellent and intentionally diverse institution "taught me to be self-disciplined in the way I learn and in the way I will teach." Maria stated that the intentional diversity of the institution "has significantly influenced my teaching practices and shaped my understanding of meeting the needs of a diverse population of students in my future classrooms."

> In accordance with the core values of the college, the teacher candidates embrace working with a diverse community of learners. Responses from all four teacher candidates indicated that they welcome diverse learners in their classrooms.

References

White, M. C., & Bembenutty, H. (2013). Not all avoidance help seekers are created equal individual differences in adaptive and executive help seeking. *SAGE Open, 3*(2), 1–14. doi:10.1177/2158244013484916.

Zimmerman, B. J., & Pons, M. M. (1986). Development of a structured interview for assessing student use of self-regulated learning strategies. *American Educational Research Journal, 23*(4), 614–628.

Chapter 7
Putting It All Together: What Really Matters?

> *It is highly suggested that K-12 teachers and college instructors use instructional time to provide students with the appropriate information that could reap important benefits in both the short term as well as help-seeking skills relevant for life-long learning, especially given an information environment that increasingly places demands for such skills.*
>
> Karabenick and Berger (2013, p. 255)

Abstract This chapter highlights the major findings of this case study in which we followed four teacher candidates from student teaching until 2 years after graduation. This chapter also highlights the major contributions of this case study with regard to the important role self-regulation of learning plays in teacher preparation programs. The case study revealed that teacher candidates from diverse backgrounds and disadvantaged conditions could be effective teachers if they have training on self-regulation and have a strong support from an institution, instructors, and peers. By focusing on cutting-edge theoretical and empirical work, this final chapter reveals that institutional support, teacher educators' commitment to mentor aspiring teachers, and peer support matter in the training and development of aspiring teachers. This chapter calls all teacher educators to implement educational systems conducive to promote self-regulation of learning among teacher candidates who, in order to be effective teachers, need first to understand that they need to be effective learners.

Keywords Self-regulation · Self-efficacy · Help seeking · Intrinsic motivation · Social cognitive theory · Delay of gratification

In this book, we examined the teaching experiences of four teacher candidates during practical and clinical experiences in urban classroom settings. Our investigation was guided by the tenets of social cognitive theory (Bandura 1977, 1997) and self-regulation of learning theory (Zimmerman 2004, 2013). Specifically, we investigated the association between self-regulatory and motivational tendencies in the context of a teacher preparation program with an emphasis on teacher self-efficacy,

© The Author(s) 2015
H. Bembenutty et al., *Developing Self-regulation of Learning and Teaching Skills Among Teacher Candidates*, SpringerBriefs in Education,
DOI 10.1007/978-94-017-9950-8_7

help seeking, and academic delay of gratification. In addition, we examined the association between self-regulatory skills and motivational beliefs in the context of the student teaching experience. The methods we chose to use included a survey in the form of a questionnaire (completed by teacher candidates during their student teaching experience), structured interviews, and classroom observations. We began with a review of the literature pertaining to teacher candidates training within the framework of the social cognitive and self-regulated theories with particular emphasis to underrepresented teacher candidates from urban communities. We then described the specific findings from the study and presented them holistically in the form of a case study.

In general, the results revealed that teacher candidates who have positive attitudes towards self-regulation, self-efficacy beliefs, delay of gratification, and positive help-seeking tendencies were those who reported high teacher self-efficacy beliefs and engaged frequently in help seeking when it was necessary (Bembenutty 2006; Bembenutty and White 2013). In addition, teacher candidates with a positive attitude towards help seeking and self-regulation were those who preferred to delay gratification and evidenced high self-efficacy.

We uncovered that for the four teacher candidates, self-regulation was important for their academic success and teaching preparation training (Bembenutty and Chen 2005). In addition, self-regulation, help seeking, academic delay of gratification, and self-efficacy appear to buffer the teaching preparation training of teacher candidates who were initially at risk for completing the program. Positive environment, caring educators, supportive peers, institutional core values, and departmental philosophy were elements that fostered self-regulation of learning among these four teacher candidates from diverse backgrounds. In this general discussion, we first summarize the findings in four different subsections: motivational findings, cognitive findings, resource management findings, and contextual or environmental findings.

7.1 Major Findings: Motivation

For these four teacher candidates, their motivation was a key determinant to remaining focused and on track during their student teaching experience and future accomplishments.

Self-efficacy beliefs for learning and for teaching were strong motivators for these four teacher candidates (Bandura 1997; Tschannen-Moran and Hoy 2001; Zimmerman 1990, 1998). Beliefs about their capabilities and competencies helped them to execute specific tasks under the most challenging conditions. These beliefs were implanted in them by their college instructors and encouraged by their cooperating teachers and peers. The cooperative environment in the college created a sense of collective self-efficacy, which was nurtured over their time at the institution and is observable in their current professions as teachers and as a legal specialist. Even when these teacher candidates experienced language, financial, and educational challenges, their self-efficacy helped them persevere with considerable effort when faced with overwhelming obstacles. Consistent with the social cognitive theory, these finding support Robbins et al.'s (2004) findings that self-efficacy was the strongest predictor of GPA. Specifically, all four students indicated that self-efficacy helped them to obtain high levels of academic success and achievement.

Perseverance requires *intrinsic motivation* (Deci 1975; Deci and Ryan 1985), a component of the forethought phase of self-regulation that maintains engagement in the task for the sake of the task. Based on their interviews and classroom observations, it is evident that the four teacher candidates were intrinsically motivated. All four teacher candidates reported that the teacher preparation courses and student teaching experiences were interesting, satisfying, and enjoyable to them. In addition, those who are employed as teachers indicate they encourage their students to pursue intrinsically motivating activities to balance work that does not have the same rewards.

All four teacher candidates in the case study discovered the importance of *goal setting* during their teacher preparation (Zimmerman et al. 1994, 1996). Setting meaningful and proximal goals directed them to select appropriate strategies that could assist them in reaching those goals. Given their socioeconomic challenges, they could have easily chosen to redirect their efforts away from goal attainment; however, they remained focused on the high expectation they placed on attaining those goals and remained in the program. They were motivated to attain both their outcome goals (e.g., graduation, teaching profession) and their process goals (e.g., selection of short-term and attainable goals) in a specific time frame. Goals consistently guided their actions and when they realized that their goals were set to high or their performance were off-track, they went to their instructors, peers, and other faculty members for help (Paris and Paris 2001).

7.2 Major Findings: Cognition

Organizational skills were a continued trademark of these four teacher candidates who attributed their ability to be highly organized to the modeling and instruction received during their years in the teacher preparation program. Training in becoming a highly effective teacher included methods to prioritize tasks, organize information, sequentially lesson plan, and manage multiple tasks. Often during student teaching, they made appointments with their instructors to seek help with organizing their lesson plans. As help seekers, they understood that they needed assistance in order to master organizational skills. *Metacognitive self-regulation* was another cognitive process in which they engaged (Garcia and Pintrich 1996; Pintrich 1999; Pintrich and De Groot 1990). It was very evident during the interview and the classroom observations that the four teacher candidates benefitted from reflecting on how they applied teaching and learning strategies to their performance. They cited examples of how they avoided distractions and remained focused on the tasks. By setting and monitoring goals, the four teacher candidates adjusted their methods of learning difficult material and received coaching on how to deliver challenging lessons (Boekaerts 1997; Boekaerts and Niemivirta 2000).

7.3 Major Findings: Resource Management

The four teacher candidates demonstrated that they engaged in *control of time and study environment* as two self-regulatory strategies (Garcia and Pintrich 1996; Pintrich 1999; Pintrich and De Groot 1990; Pintrich et al. 1993). They remained task-focused, made effective use of study time, and adhered to predetermined schedules. They also learned the high benefits of *adaptive help seeking* (Karabenick and Newman 2006; White 2010; Volet and Karabenick 2006), which they used to strategically direct their goal attainment by seeking help from knowledgeable sources such as faculty, peers, or media outlets in order to facilitate their learning when faced with obstacles. Certainly, the four teacher candidates were experts in seeking help from their instructors and cooperating teachers, but they needed to learn how to refine their skills to seek help from technological sources and from peers.

Academic delay of gratification was another learning strategy that these teacher candidates understood was an important contributor to their academic success and effective teaching. According to Bembenutty (2010); Bembenutty and Karabenick (1998, 2004), the ability to delay gratification is the cornerstone of all academic achievement and education. He asserts that it is by delaying gratification that learners can pursue long-term academic and career goals. These teacher candidates provided evidence that delaying gratification during their teaching training was accomplished by postponing immediately available rewards in order to complete a difficult project or study for a state certification exam. However, during the interview, they had difficulty explaining how they could help their own students delay gratification. This is an area new to the educational arena, and teacher educators might consider dedicating time to instill in their students the need to incorporate this important self-regulatory strategy.

7.4 Major Findings: Academic Environment

In addition to findings in the areas of motivational, cognitive, and resource management, academic environment findings are presented in this case study. The identification of what makes up an academic environment includes factors which are external to the learner (Weinstein and Acee 2013). These academic environmental factors include: the resources available to the learner, instructor expectations, nature of the learning activity, and the nature of the social context and the level of social support (Weinstein and Acee 2013). These four teacher candidates had limited financial support, but they received strong support from their college, peers, and instructors. They were protected by a strong social support system and could attribute their successes and achievements to some extent to that support. These four teacher candidates were taught by advisors and faculty who helped them to acquire knowledge, provided supplemental instructional materials, and were available by email and cell phone when needed. Their instructors' expectations remained consistently high for all four teacher candidates to achieve their academic and behavioral goals, and these instructors remained available beyond their graduation from the program.

7.5 What Is Significant About This Case Study?

Working closely with these four teacher candidates for several years has given us a platform from which we can suggest important changes for programs that prepare teachers. Questions such as: How did the college administration contribute to the success of these teacher candidates? What personal attributes were critical to these teacher candidates' successful completion of the teacher education program? In addition, we reflect about what we believe to be the most significant contributing factors to the academic success and achievement of these four teacher candidates and in fact, to any other teacher candidate enrolled in a teacher preparation program.

7.5.1 College Environment

Administrative support matters. The academic and personal successes of these four teacher candidates are undoubtedly an outcome of the strong core values held by the institution where they were enrolled. As it was discussed at the beginning of the book, the core values are social relevance, academic excellence, global engagement, intentional diversity, and personal transformation. The case study represents how the college intentionally implements these core values. For instance, with regard to being academically excellent, the college maintains the highest academic accreditations with a sense of humility. Being intentionally diverse, the college provides educational access and support to motivated students from diverse ethnic, cultural, and socioeconomic backgrounds.

The college has remained open to diverse learners such as the teacher candidates in this study who are of Hispanic heritage, are second language learners, and have diverse socioeconomic backgrounds. The college provided them an opportunity to excel, but the students were active learners who made individual commitments to the core values upon admission. The level of commitment from the administration made a significant difference in their completion of the teacher education program requirements, and, we argue, this type of commitment is a model for future teacher candidates.

Teacher educators support matters. Another protective factor in the pursuit of academic dreams and a teaching profession for these teacher candidates was the strong support they consistently received from their teacher educators. The caring nature of their educators mattered tremendously for the teacher candidates. The teacher educators were charismatic, maintained effective classroom management, had high expectations, and they were excellent role models of what a teacher should be. The teacher candidates admired and respected their educators who played multiple unofficial roles such as mentors, counselors at time of adversity, and spiritual guides. They trusted their educators and relied on them for academic as well as for personal advice. Certainly, these positive interactions, support, and professional relations mattered significantly for these four teacher candidates.

Peer support matters. In response to the positive environment the college and the teacher educators provided, teacher candidates readily supported each other's academic efforts. Often the support came in the form of encouragement; however, when needed, the teacher candidates challenged each other to increase time on task to improve their performance. In some ways, the teacher candidates became a family, often taking on the roles of brothers and sisters. To increase their chances of successfully completing a task or studying for an exam, they would study together and share resources. In addition, they led chapel together and even had fun together. When one of them needed support during a time of personal or educational challenges, the others were there to provide help, assistance, and also to serve as peer mentors who instilled self-efficacy belief. They served as co-regulators. Peer support mattered significantly for these teacher candidates.

A rigorous teaching program matters. Another factor that significantly influenced the successes experienced by these four teacher candidates was the rigorous teaching preparation program the college maintains. Teacher candidates were consistently mentored, advised, counseled, and received one to one tutoring throughout their teacher training. Student teaching placements were intentionally selected to be the best fit for each teacher candidate and the learning environment. Monitoring by school-based teachers and administration was an important source of feedback for the college faculty and student teaching supervisors. Full time instructors were, for the most part, the clinical experience supervisors and these supervisors together brought more than 40 years of teaching proficiency and clinical practice in diverse settings. As a result of the School of Education's partnership with the schools that received their student teachers, there exists partnerships that have fostered strong connections and relationships between the teacher educators and the cooperating teachers. As reported by the four teacher candidates, the rigorous teaching programs had a strong effect on their training to be successful teachers.

Culturally proactive pedagogy matters. The intentionality of the institution to welcome culturally diverse learners was very evident during the observations and interviews portions of the case study. The four teacher candidates felt at home when they were on a campus even with teacher educators who did not have similar backgrounds or life experiences. The institution and program celebrate equity and diversity while maintaining a rigorous program. Understanding diversity in the schools and in the program was a paramount factor contributing to the success of the teacher candidates. The environment and social interactions were constant reminders that teacher candidates were important and unique individuals who had some particular strength to bring to the program. A celebration of the differences provided a venue where teacher candidates were valued contributors, regardless of their socioeconomic background, ethnicity, language, or educational experiences. The cultural openness of this environment was successful in a significant way because it integrated a form of self-regulation of learning in which learners were not only *culturally responsive,* but also proactive learners. With regard to the successes of these four teacher candidates, a *culturally proactive pedagogy* mattered.

7.5.2 Personal Commitment

Self-regulation matters. Academic and professional success cannot only depend on external factors; personal commitment matters too (Randi et al. 2011). Self-regulation of learning was a pivotal factor in the success of these four teacher candidates and made a significant difference in the ways in which these teacher candidates were able to deal with challenges and overcome obstacles. Certainly, these teacher candidates did not respond identically to their teacher training; learners respond in different ways based on their prior experiences, values, beliefs, and cultural backgrounds. Regardless of their differences, self-regulation was an observable behavior manifested through their motivation, use of strategies, and beliefs in spite of challenges. They took control of their learning, set short- and long-term goals, engaged in planning, and monitored their progress (Schunk 2001, 2003; Schunk and Pajares 2009; Schunk and Zimmerman 1997, 2007).

Self-efficacy for learning and teaching matter. Consistent with the social cognitive theory, self-efficacy beliefs are a fundamental factor in human agency. These teacher candidates empowered themselves with self-efficacy beliefs that generated effort, perseverance, and continued commitment even when facing obstacles. From observing and interviewing the teacher candidates, it was evident that, consistent with Bandura's social cognitive theory, they acquired self-efficacy beliefs from their teacher educators who used verbal prompts, modeling, vicarious learning, and peer learning to instill competence and self-beliefs. By providing training in specific self-regulatory skills, and flooding the environment with phrases that are known to raise self-efficacy the teacher educators set in motion a method that the teacher candidates could use to monitor their self-efficacy for each task. For example, phrases from teacher educators and peers enhanced the self-efficacy beliefs of these teacher candidates. These phrases included encouragement such as, "You can do it," "You have mastered a similar task before and you can master this one because it is very similar to the previous one," "I believe in you," and "We can help you," (Pajares 1996; Tschannen-Moran and Hoy 2001; Usher and Pajares 2008).

Adaptive help seeking matters. Help seeking is a self-regulatory learning strategy useful to sustaining goal-directed plans. It is also a behavior and a social strategy. Help seeking places the responsibility to become active agents in directing their learning and professional aspirations on individual learners (Newman 1998). A hallmark evidenced in this case study was that the self-worth of these teacher candidates was not threatened by having to seek help. They did not avoid seeking help to maintain their independence, and they only solicited help when needed to move forward with a specific task. The teacher educators in this program removed the stigma that can be associated with help seeking early on in the program, and emphasized the multiple venues at the college where help is available when needed. However, help seeking was incorporated into the curriculum by teaching the four teacher candidates how to seek help strategically. The teacher educators were convinced teacher candidates needed to be competent and resolute in mastering help seeking (Karabenick 2004; Karabenick and Berger 2013; Karabenick and Newman 2006; Nelson-Le Gall 1981; Volet and Karabenick 2006; White 2010).

Academic delay of gratification matters. This case study highlighted the importance of the association between academic delay of gratification, learners' motivational beliefs, and use of self-regulatory learning strategies. Academic delay of gratification matters for learners in general, but specifically for teacher candidates. The ability to forego immediately available and attractive alternatives was a cornerstone in these four teacher candidates. They learned to postpone obtaining an attractive income until after graduation and were able to decline invitations to parties when lesson plans needed to be done. They practiced perseverance, persistence in the face of obstacles, and were deliberate in their choices. Keeping logs, writing in weekly planners, monitoring progress, and reflecting on outcomes helped these teacher candidates to overcome barriers and following graduation, reach their long term goal of becoming teachers (Bandura and Mischel 1965; Bembenutty 2006, 2013; Bembenutty and Karabenick 1998, 2004; Mischel 2014).

7.6 Limitations of the Case Study

The case study provides an important empirical assessment of the trajectories of the participants beginning with their initial steps into student teaching and ending 2 years following their graduation with reports of their current career status. As in all case study research, it is important to note that the one described by the researchers in this book has several limitations. First, the sample size of the case study used to present the results of the research is very small. Nevertheless, the methodology used was comprehensive and by triangulating the data, we were able to successfully report consistency of the findings across multiple measures. Second, there is only one male teacher candidate in the study; therefore, generalization to other male teacher candidates needs to be done with caution.

Third, the participants were attending a faith-based institution, and all four teacher candidates professed a strong religious faith. At the college, there are opportunities to voluntarily attend and participate in chapel services and receive spiritual support from the Dean of Students; therefore, it is unknown if teacher candidates' conscientious efforts came from spiritual and faith-based sources and if faculty's commitment to the teacher candidates' success came from their spiritual beliefs. Therefore, results might be different in institutions where teacher candidates and instructors do not profess a strong faith-based mission. Although the participants' religious beliefs are not considered a limitation, we make the reader aware of the intentionality of the institution to consider while evaluating whether or not it is an important factor in the processes and outcomes of the study. Fourth, the researchers were not able to formally observe the four participants after they completed their education training.

7.7 Educational Implications

The case study presents findings that can inspire teacher education programs to remain committed to working with students who would not at first glance be eligible for admission. Taking into consideration the under representation of minority teachers in both the classroom and the teacher education pipeline, the results of this study support working with students who aspire to be teachers and could fill that void. Much consideration has been given to linking the search for highly qualified teachers to high school GPA and SAT scores. Currently, teacher education programs need to fill their teacher candidate pool with students who will predictably pass the new state examinations or fear losing their status as licensing programs. As a result, some teacher education programs across the country may be closing their doors to the under prepared students who if given the appropriate tools and support, could become the most highly qualified teachers to work in high needs areas with the growing population of at-risk students.

There is a possible answer to the question that never ceases to go away, "Why are there not more minority teachers in classrooms across the United States?" It is not for the lack of aspiring teachers in the population; the number of minorities who state their intention to enter teacher education programs dissipates by 50 % throughout the 4–5 year stint. Access to a teacher education programs is based on whether the candidate has the potential to pass the certification exams. Across the United States of America, researchers have reported lower scores for minority teacher candidates than for non-minority candidates (Epstein 2005; McIntosh and Norwood 2004), which result in the under representation of minority teachers in the classroom.

The issue is no longer whether or not to accept underprepared college applicants, but how to identify and assist them. Arguments that support relaxing admission's standards include maximizing educational opportunity to give students a chance to show what they can do. This argument is supported by the results of the case study. The insufficient number of certified minority teachers poses a great threat to many areas of education such as inner city schools. African-American,

Hispanic, and Native American teachers are more likely to work in schools with minority populations and low-income families than their White counterparts. Consequently, a decrease in the numbers of teachers from these groups is likely to mean fewer strong role models for students living in low-income, low-performing schools (Bennett 2002; Keller 2007).

7.8 What Can Be Done?

The implications of this study address the problem facing the teacher workforce across America: how to attract, prepare, and retain teachers in high poverty urban schools (Boyd et al. 2006). A primary place to seek minority teaching candidates is among those who already reside in a particular urban area and will effectively teach urban children (Haberman 2000). However, in order to tap this pool of potential minority teachers, educators must take into account the learning experiences of these teacher candidates prior to college. These students require programs that address their personal as well as their academic needs. Many African American and Latino students are either first-generation college attendees or older students whose families have little or no prior experience with the demands of college. They are striving to be the first college graduates in their families (Gonzalez 1997). Caldwell and Siwatu (2003) identify important areas of weakness that limit minority students' success in college; specifically, they observed that students who lack effective *help-seeking strategies* enter college with a disadvantage. Caldwell and Siwatu (2003) surveyed pre-college initiative programs that were successful in transitioning under prepared high school students to college. Along with their development of cognitive learning skills (Gordon 1999), minority students need training in social learning skills, such as help-seeking and delaying gratification, to succeed in college environments. In addition, they also could benefit from consistent monitoring of their self-efficacy for learning and teacher efficacy.

Research studies on the inclusion of "at risk" college students have provided evidence that self-regulated learning processes are significantly related to academic success for this population (Ley and Young 1998). A distinguish characteristic between "at risk" and regular admission college students is the way they plan, organize, monitor, evaluate, and think about the learning process (Carr et al. 1991). A more holistic consideration of what would actually help students from impoverished educational settings considers the importance of hiring teachers who comes from similar educational settings; however, the pool for this teacher candidate is small. Based on these case study findings, an environment rich in nurturing and encouragement that includes training in self-regulated learning with academic rigor will attract and retain more minority and underprepared students than one that only provides academic and financial support. Further educational implications focus on the role of the faculty and administration of teacher education programs in promoting attention and retaining teacher candidates.

7.9 Self-regulation and the Teacher Candidate

Based on the model used in the case study, there is room for teacher education program coordinators to become increasingly more subjective when evaluating the applications of at-risk teacher candidates. Those in charge of admission to these programs should carefully evaluate each applicant's prior educational experience and if appropriate, attribute prior failures to poorly constructed learning environments rather than disinterest in schooling or lack of motivation. Accounting for the impact of the interactive influences of environmental, individual, and contextual factors, teacher training programs can address deficits in underprepared teacher candidates by embedding training in self-regulation learning strategies into the instructional and clinical elements of teacher preparation.

Training teacher candidates in self-regulation requires input and monitoring from organized, self-regulated instructors, clinical supervisors, and support staff, and considerable support from the college community. The case study demonstrates how a small, yet unified teacher education program, with the help of tutors, faculty members, and funding from the college, can effectively train teacher candidates to become proactive learners and take charge of their learning. Taking into account the learners' thoughts, beliefs, feelings, and emotions while pursuing academic goals is one strategic approach to overcoming obstacles to learning. However, it all begins with faculty members who believe all students can learn and that they as instructors have the efficacy to teach those who struggle due to past failures or poor preparation. If we take these implications further, we can assert that all teacher candidates can benefit from training on self-regulated learning because students are often self-regulated in one area of their academics and not others. In addition, we can surmise that deficiencies in teacher candidate's learning strategies can interfere with their ability to successfully teach their future students how to learn thus making the case for a self-regulated learning environment for all teacher candidates.

7.10 If You Want a Better Student, Be a Better Teacher!

From the researcher's perspective, a significant educational implication drawn from the case study findings is the roles of teacher educators and administrators who are in charge of what happens in teacher education classrooms and programs. There is enough evidence in the literature that it takes a self-regulated teacher to produce a self-regulated student (Dembo 2001; White 2011b). Teacher educators can be empowered to prioritize training their teacher candidates to be self-regulated learners while training them to be teachers (Randi 2004). Dembo (2001) suggested that educational psychology courses should have two complementary goals for future teachers. The first goal is to teach future teachers to become more effective learners and the second goal is to teach them to be more effective teachers.

In the case study, the student teachers were asked questions that can also be posed to teacher educators. The case study provides a model of what teacher educators can do to provide learning environments where self-regulation and self-efficacy are as important as learning how to teach. Taking a proactive and strategic approach to working with at-risk teacher candidates can lead to an increase in the number of minority teacher candidates completing their certification programs and graduating from college. The researchers outline the following educational implications by identifying the role of the teacher educator as an active model for teacher candidates. Their actions, behaviors, and personal beliefs towards the teacher candidates will determine how their teacher candidates will view and teach their future students.

7.11 The Role of the Teacher Educator

1. How does the teacher educator perceive new teacher candidates? Does the teacher educator believe all students can learn?

How teacher educators perceive their students is a significant factor in determining their own levels of teacher efficacy. Perception of their students' abilities to progress successfully through the education pipeline influences how a teacher educator advises, plans instruction, and monitors progress. Believing all students can learn requires teacher educators to make sure that they are aware of the diversity amongst their teacher candidates. This includes their prior educational experiences, cultural differences, learning challenges, language difficulties, and whatever other obstacles there might be to their learning. Planning and instruction include pedagogy in the value of setting and attaining proximal goals so students can see their progress quickly and move forward to the next goal attainment with increased self-efficacy.

2. Does the teacher educator believe teacher candidates have responsibilities in the classroom? What are they? What are the teacher educator's responsibilities for teacher candidates' learning to increase?

Directing teacher candidates to focus on "how they learn" before they "learn how to teach" leads to a shared responsibility between the teacher educator and the teacher candidate for outcomes. Before teacher candidates become proactive and take charge of their learning, they need to realize that learning is not something that happens "to" them, but it is an area that can be managed using self-regulation and learning strategies. However, the teacher educator is the model, and the teacher candidate is the observer for a substantial period of time. The model remains present and available until the behaviors observed in the model can be emulated, practiced, and then performed independently. For students who struggle to remain in the teacher education pipeline, the consistent presence of a model who slowly and deliberately removes himself/herself from the process is essential to their successful completion of the program.

3. *How confident is the teacher educator that teacher candidates will complete the teaching? Can the teacher educator motivate all learners? Does the teacher educator have all the necessary skills to help at-risk aspiring teachers? What is the teacher educator's role as related to teacher candidates' learning experience? How much of their learning depends on the teacher educator in regard to their academic achievement?*

Teacher efficacy is a significant factor in motivating teacher candidates to devote the amount of time and effort required to complete a teacher education program successfully. In addition to doing well in education courses, there are clinical hours, content courses, and teacher certification exams to be completed. Students who enter the teacher education pipeline often become discouraged by the overwhelming demands of the courses, and their self-efficacy for learning and teaching decreases significantly. The self-regulated and highly efficacious teacher educators follow the cyclical phases of self-regulation as they mentor each student, guiding them through the phases of forethought, performance, and self-reflection (DiBenedetto and White 2013). Following Zimmerman's model of self-regulation, the teacher educator guides each teacher candidate to set proximal goals, checks to see if the goals are being met, and reflects on how the goals were attained or not attained. By putting this model in place for each task, the teacher takes on the role of mentor, not instructor, allowing the teacher candidates to take responsibility for their own progress, but remaining involved providing feedback, correct misconceptions, and providing help when requested.

4. *How does a teacher educator teach self-regulation?*

First, the teacher educator has to be motivated to model self-regulated behaviors in and out of the classroom. In order to teach self-regulation, the teacher educator has to be self-regulated, replacing traditional instructional planning methods with goals linked to specific actions that are monitored and reflected upon to see how those goals are met. Relying on feedback from their students, teacher educators can gather important information about their own teaching and make adjustments to better meet the needs of their teacher candidates. We no longer have a one size fits all way of shaping teacher candidates into successful and certified teachers. The pipeline is crowded with demands from accreditation boards and state certification requirements that require teacher educators to maintain high levels of teacher efficacy for easily overwhelmed teacher candidates.

Dembo (2001) designed an educational psychology course to help teacher candidates develop essential self-regulatory skills. The elements of the course provide the teacher educator with a framework from which to teach self-regulation to teacher candidates so they in turn will eventually teach these same skills to students in school classrooms. Teacher candidates first study the theory and research related to the self-regulatory dimensions. Second, they are asked to examine their own motivation and learning beliefs regarding specific dimensions. Third, they practice using the strategies related to each self-regulatory dimension within the context of their role as students in a teacher preparation program. Finally, they consider how they can teach their future students how to apply the strategies to their own learning.

Following Zimmerman (1998), White and DiBenedetto (2015) recommend a model that integrates strategies that can help high school students become managers of the areas that so often negatively impact their performance. This model can be applied to teacher candidates. For instance, teacher candidates who answer questions about when they will do the task (time management), what they will do to get task done (behavior), where they will do the task (physical environment), why they will do the task (motivation), how they will get task done (method), and with whom they will do the task (selective use of resources) are consistently engaging in self-monitoring. Self-regulation includes the monitoring of basic psychological functioning, such as motivation (why we do it), method (how we do it), and time (when we do it) (Zimmerman 1998). Asking teacher candidates to take more responsibility for managing their own learning requires lining up teaching and learning methods with self-regulation dimensions to bridge the gaps now in place (see Table 7.1).

5. *What efforts can teacher educators make to recognize strategic help seeking and help avoidance?*

Many teacher educators model help seeking as a strategy in their classrooms without realizing it. Yet, many of their students do not vicariously adopt these strategies because there is still a stigma associated with seeking help especially for teacher candidates. Teacher candidates often see themselves as future teachers and fall into patterns of help avoidance rather than admit they need assistance in the academic or clinical setting. White and Bembenutty (2013) conducted a study with teacher candidates' use of help-seeking strategies in the context of preparing for state certification exams. The results revealed that students' tendencies for help seeking vary according to their goal tendencies, teacher self-efficacy beliefs, and use of self-regulatory strategies, such as delay of gratification. These findings suggest that help seeking is indeed a self-regulatory learning strategy used by learners to pursue valuable academic goals.

Educators who train teacher candidates to become successful classroom teachers should work toward dispelling the stigmas associated with help seeking at the earliest opportunity. Often, when a learner weighs the costs and benefits of seeking help, the consequences of revealing weakness puts at risk the appearance of competence and can result in the choice to avoid any appearance of incompetence. In some cases, delaying gratification can be linked to help avoidance; the learner's desire to appear competent can be associated with maintaining social status. Teacher educators can remove the stigma from seeking help by identifying it as a self-regulatory learning strategy that is used by successful learners. They can also train teacher candidates in adaptive help-seeking strategies by identifying resources and provide opportunities for teacher candidates to work cooperatively rather than individually for specific goal attainment.

6. *How can teacher educators guide teacher candidates toward becoming self-regulated in the college courses and clinical settings?*

Teacher educators can encourage the use of self-monitoring tools to raise teacher candidates' awareness of how their thoughts, feelings, and actions impact their performance for various tasks. Homework logs have been found to be

Table 7.1 Dimensions of academic self-regulation and teacher educator responsibilities

Criteria	Psychological dimensions	Task conditions	Self-regulatory attributes	Self-regulatory processes	Teacher educator
When	Time	Set time limits	Timely, efficient delay of gratification	Time management	Raise teacher candidates' awareness of time constraints and social interferences for completing specific projects, preparing for state certification exams, fulfilling clinical hour requirements, and other course deadlines
What	Behavior	Set goal for outcome behavior	Self-awareness	Self-monitoring, self-evaluation	Raise teacher candidates' awareness of behaviors that lead to becoming self-regulated teacher candidates
Where	Physical environment	Structure environment	Environmentally sensitive/resourceful	Environmental structuring	Promote environmental awareness amongst teacher candidates by reinforcing good choices and poor choices of studying venues
Why	Motive	Choose to participate	Self-motivated	Goal setting and self-efficacy	Model and supervise setting of proximal goals that lead to goal attainment over a shorter period of time and raise self-efficacy among teacher candidates
How	Method	Choose method	Planned or routinized	Task strategies, self-instruction	Provide opportunities for teacher candidates to demonstrate comprehension of subject under investigation
With whom?	Social	Choose partner, model, or teacher	Socially sensitive and resourceful	Selective help seeking and resource management	Mentor teacher candidates by helping them narrow or broaden help seeking using resources appropriate to support their learning

helpful tools of self-monitoring for students across grade levels and curriculums. Researchers have begun to apply the cyclical process to homework assignments using homework logs and diaries (Schmitz et al. 2011; Schmitz and Wiese 2006). According to Zimmerman, Bonner, and Kovach (1996), homework logs are helpful to record self-monitoring progress of homework tasks, record goals and strategies for completing homework, and to record beliefs, track help seeking, and evaluation of outcomes. Zimmerman et al. (1996) developed a theoretical model of homework self-regulation using homework logs in which learners could record homework goals, time when assignments started and were completed, where and with whom assignments were completed, and the learners' level of self-efficacy beliefs.

Successful homework completion also encompasses learners' ability to delay gratification and seek help from appropriate sources. *Help seeking* is an important self-regulatory strategy associated with academic achievement and assignment completion (Bembenutty and White 2013; Karabenick and Berger 2013; White 2011a, b).

While completing homework assignments, there is evidence of the influence of motivational beliefs such as self-efficacy and intrinsic motivation, self-regulatory processes, and use of help-seeking strategies, which are associated with homework completion (Bembenutty 2010). Teacher educators can assist teacher candidates by encouraging the use of homework logs, making time to provide feedback by checking their entries, and helping them adapt the behaviors that led to poor performance.

7. *How can teacher educators help teacher candidates to delay gratification for the sake of learning?*

Teacher candidates beyond those represented in the case study have participated in studies that included delay of gratification. To remain task-focused when completing homework or doing other types of academic tasks, students also need to engage in *academic delay of gratification* (Bembenutty 2010) which refers to postponing immediate, available rewards for the sake of pursuing more valuable and temporarily distant rewards. Many teacher candidates are distracted by social media and have difficulty making the correct choice to maintain a strict study schedule rather than meet with friends or as in the case study students, volunteer in their communities. Teacher educators can help teacher candidates by focusing on the process rather than the outcome of academic and clinical tasks. When teacher educators focus on the outcome of homework assignments, they may overlook the beliefs, motivation, and self-reflection processes that influenced task completion. Understanding this process may help teacher educators to enhance teacher candidates' perception of their own performance.

7.12 The Role of the Teacher Candidate

The case study represents what can happen when teacher candidates are equal participants in the process of becoming self-regulated learners, using adapted help-seeking strategies, and delaying gratification in order to graduate from the teacher education program. Teacher educators can encourage their teacher candidates to self-monitor, use homework logs, incorporate help-seeking strategies, and delay gratification; however if the teacher candidate is not motivated to participate, the results are poor. Academic and clinical environments make similar demands on both teachers and teacher candidates. It is the teacher educator's role to model, and the teacher candidate's response is to learn from the model. Bandura describe four interrelated components of vicarious learning: attentional, retentional, motoric reproduction, and observational reinforcement processes. The teacher candidate is expected to participate fully in each process.

- The *attentional process* involves a person observing a model's experience so as to learn from the model such as the teacher candidate making himself available to seek out and work with competent models to improve his performance in class, on state exams, or in his clinical experience.
- The *retentional process* involves remembering what the model(s) did over a period of time. The teacher candidate is intentional in practicing and following strategies modeled for him by his teacher educator, clinical supervisor, or peers, throughout the entire teacher education preparation program. By sharing what he has observed with his peers, or during clinical practice, the teacher candidate verbally reinforces the self-regulated strategies he has observed from his teacher educator.
- The *motoric reproduction* involves mastering what has been observed and practiced. The teacher candidate is responsible to apply self-regulated learning strategies, help seeking, and delay of gratification in areas that might not appear to be related to his teacher candidacy, yet are important factors in maintaining the required GPA, passing certification exams, and demonstrating the habits of a highly effective teacher in clinical settings.
- The *observational reinforcement* process involves connecting observed behaviors to a positive or negative reaction or outcome. Teacher candidates are more likely to incorporate learned and mastered strategies if the outcomes lead to successful attainment of their goals. When teacher candidates use self-monitoring tools such as homework or study logs, they are able to track their progress and attribute outcomes to their strategy use during specific tasks. Attributions to effort rather than external influences can provide teacher candidates with insight into their personal learning practices and help them make adaptations for future tasks.

Requiring the teacher candidate to fully appreciate the power of human agency and his ability to control his thoughts, feelings, and actions is a significant part of the process of proactive learning. The case study results represent what happens when at-risk learners from minority populations are part of a greater learning community that invites them to be full participants in their educational experiences. The teacher candidates did not enter the institution qualified to meet the standards of any teacher education program, yet they all succeeded in completing the program requirements to graduate from the college. Further educational implications for educators who are interested in training at-risk, aspiring teacher candidates to become teachers include the effectiveness of seeking and obtaining assistance, specifically for students who could become isolated and persisting towards academic failure. Many who have failed to continue in the teacher education pipeline have left due to past experiences that impacted their ability to meet the standards of rigorous teacher education programs. Future aspiring teachers could benefit from close monitoring by caring and nurturing teacher educators who are motivated to embed self-regulated learning into their teacher preparation programs.

7.13 Where Are We Heading from Here?

The four teacher candidates remained in contact with the teacher educators beyond their completion of the teacher preparation program. The college has a strong alumni association that maintains relationships with its graduates through social networking, professional workshops, and invitations to speak with current teacher candidates. All four participants are working in professional settings, three as teachers and one as a legal assistant. They report they are satisfied with their current standings in their professions, and they often use self-regulatory strategies to remain successful. For example, all participants report using organizational and time management strategies and continue to seek help when needed. They often share how their self-efficacy beliefs acquired during their time in the program have transferred to their new professions.

Three of the four participants applied and were accepted to graduate school at the same institution where they obtained their teaching degrees. Two of them obtained their Master's degrees in special education with a second licensure. The third participant obtained a Master's degree in Teaching of English to Speakers of Other Language (TESOL) with a second licensure. The fourth participant moved to another state and has not yet completed a graduate degree but is working towards a Master's degree in Literacy.

7.14 Chris

His student teaching experience in a school where English Language Acquisition is a primary goal inspired Chris to seek a position in a school that needed bilingual teachers. Before interviewing for that position, Chris sought out the advice of his college advisor asking for input regarding a lesson presentation. That decision made him more aware of student needs, and as a result, he pursued a Master's degree in TESOL instead of Literacy and now is certified to teach K-12 English Language Learners and Childhood Education. Given how he distinguished himself in the graduate program as an excellent teacher, the director invited him to lead workshops for adult second language learners. He also returned to the college to instruct teacher candidates in literacy assessment. In addition, he is actively involved in the community by providing homework help for parents and children who are English language learners. Chris is the director of the ESL program in his school and will return to college to get credits in Bilingual Education.

7.15 Maria

Her student teaching experience in a private school where access to special education resources were limited led her to pursue a Master's degree in Special Education. Her passion to teach students with special needs in the traditional classroom inspired her to obtain dual certification in childhood education and special education. When preparing to be interviewed for a position in an urban charter school, Maria sought out input from the student teacher coordinator about the process and asked for help regarding her responses to specific questions which led to her being hired. This past year she was recognized by her school community for having the highest state test scores in both Mathematics and English Language Arts. After preparing her students for common core state exams, she stated, *As a result of using self-regulatory strategies to self-monitor during test preparation, my students saw their growth and felt extremely proud of themselves which removed anxiety for the state tests because they observed their progress as they practiced. All of my students passed the state exam! Not only did our class score the highest in the entire school, but none of my students failed!*

7.16 Jaime

Her student teaching experience in a small private school with state funded special education services for preschoolers gave her the opportunity to observe teaching practices specific to a special needs population. This exposure led her to accept a kindergarten position and pursue a Master's degree in Special Education. Given her exemplary progress in the Master's program, Jaime was able to obtain her special education certification and is currently teaching in an inclusive classroom. When observed by teacher candidates from the program, she presented not only her expertise in differentiated instruction, but also how she uses the self-regulatory skills acquired during the years of teacher preparation. Both her self-efficacy for learning and teacher efficacy are easily observed while she is teaching her second grade class.

7.17 Angela

Her student teaching experience in a school with a significant immigrant population increased her awareness of the challenges faced by both the parents and students to communicate with English speaking teachers and administrators. For this reason, she served as a translator during after school hours and parent conferences. While pursuing a graduate degree in Literacy and TESOL, an opportunity to work in the criminal justice system presented itself. Her experience as a translator in the school system led to a position and training opportunity with a prestigious law firm. As a legal assistant, she has been able to apply the self-regulatory learning strategies of time management, organization, and help seeking as she provides services for English language learners who are unfamiliar with the legal system. Regarding her present profession, Angela stated, *The lawyers I work for often ask why I go beyond what is required with clients, and I respond 'it is because of my experience with faculty who frequently went beyond what was required of them so I could succeed!'*

7.18 Conclusion

The case study presented in this book makes it clear that there is a link between social cognitive theory, self-regulation, and the preparation of future teachers. The interaction of personal, behavioral, and environmental factors provides a framework for drawing some conclusions from the journeys of four aspiring teachers who may not have been considered top candidates for the teaching profession. The four teacher candidates defy the statistical odds as a result of the self-regulatory approach they adopted toward successful completion of a demanding teacher preparation program, accompanied by a supportive and nurturing academic environment.

Initially, we met these teacher candidates as they endeavored to realize their dreams to become teachers. They soon learned that admission to college is not enough, their past challenges, deficiencies in their high schools, low self-efficacy, and not knowing how to seek help were obstacles to meeting the requirements to be admitted to the teacher preparation program. What they did not know, was that their choice of college would make a significant difference in their success. A desire to prepare future teachers for the most challenging learning environments led committed faculty members to intentionally embed training in self-regulation into their teacher preparation courses as the hallmark of the program. These teacher educators created a social environment that encouraged each teacher candidate to grow academically, dispositionally, and socially to reach their highest potential.

The case study results are supported by research in self-regulation, which has revealed that in practically all levels of learning enterprises, when learners engage in self-regulatory processes such as goal-setting, self-monitoring, self-evaluation, self-reflections, and help seeking, they achieve higher levels of personal, academic, and professional outcomes in diverse contexts and social domains. Based on Bandura's social cognitive theory and Zimmerman's self-regulation theory, the case study represents the four teacher candidates as agents of change who adapted to a challenging learning environment with the intention of becoming proactive learners in charge of their outcomes and environments.

The four aspiring teachers participated in specifically designed tasks that guided them through the cyclical phases of self-regulation until their behaviors reflected self-regulatory skills. The faculty and staff had a common goal that was for the teacher candidates to learn how to learn before they could learn how to teach. Most importantly, the teacher preparation program emphasized how to use the self-regulatory strategy of help seeking as a means towards succeeding when one's self-efficacy is low or when attempts at a given task are not leading towards satisfactory outcomes. In addition, exploring the link between delay of gratification and self-efficacy as two essential forces in self-directed learning captivated the four teacher candidates and led them to make associations not previously considered as part of self-regulation.

Both clinical and academic experiences of the four teacher candidates were closely examined while student teaching in an urban setting. Examining the teacher candidates' experiences through the lens of social cognitive theory provided the researchers with a framework from which to evaluate what successful learners do and how they apply specific self-regulatory strategies to their clinical experiences. In addition, the educational setting was determined to be a significant factor in the success of the four teacher candidates. The institution they attended engaged in fulfilling the model presented in its core values and the teacher candidates can attribute their growth and development as learners and teachers to the intentional mission of the college to be both academically excellent and intentionally diverse.

All four participants were from urban settings and of Hispanic heritage and completed their student teaching practicum in educational settings with a large bilingual population. They found their ability to translate for parents and teachers increased their expertise and their desire to work with children and families who were English Language Learners. The four teacher candidates were mentored by caring and supportive faculty members prior to taking education courses. Their initial college experiences reflected the institution's commitment to provide the services required to educate students from diverse socioeconomic, educational, ethnic, and cultural backgrounds.

The researchers followed each teacher candidate as they began to apply what they have learned in their courses from the college classrooms to the school classrooms. The clinical observations, self-report questionnaires, and interviews are evidence of the effectiveness of self-regulation and teacher preparation. The teacher candidates were observed during real time lessons in their student teacher placements. Acquisition of help seeking could be partially measured by when and if they looked at their cooperating teacher for support, affirmation, and guidance during the delivery of a lesson plan. The four teacher candidates were interviewed following each observation for self-reflections and attributions. Senior Seminar provided them with a forum where they could share their student teaching experiences and get feedback from peers and faculty for future lesson presentations.

Critical to the case study research was the choice of instruments to measure the variables. The researchers carefully selected measures that had high validity and reliability. Gathering data that could be triangulated was critical to the value of the findings. There are consistent, but not identical, reported patterns of beliefs, motivations, and behaviors amongst the four teacher candidates. Putting it all together points to the reality that self-regulation of learning during student teaching is an important component associated of the success of these four aspiring teachers. The transparency of the interviews reflected a sense of self-awareness and growth in self-efficacy for learning and teaching. All four teacher candidates reported that they were confident to teach all learners both content as well as self-regulatory strategies.

In sum, "if one wants a better student be a better teacher," might be too strong of a statement, but the findings indicate that teacher educators should not overlook the lower performing students when looking to recruit students with the potential to be highly effective teachers. If high school GPA's and SAT scores become the only criteria for admitting aspiring teachers to college, we are in danger of not tapping into other equally qualified potential candidates that once graduate will be ready to meet the challenges of teaching in urban settings. If teacher preparation programs close the doors to aspiring teachers who do not at first appear to have the potential to pass the state certification exams, they are in danger of removing the culturally and socially diverse experiences these teacher candidates could bring to today's urban classrooms. The standards to become a teacher in today's schools are set high but not too high for the four teacher candidates described in the case study. The results revealed the importance of evaluating and training teacher candidates in self-regulation as a means to becoming proactive, independent learners. A strong support system is a critical factor, yet, in this case it only took a few committed faculty members who aligned their teacher preparation program with the institution's core values, and acted on it to develop self-regulation of learning and teaching skills among these four teacher candidates.

References

Bandura, A. (1977). *Social learning theory*. Englewood Cliffs, NJ: Prentice Hall.

Bandura, A. (1997). *Self-efficacy: The exercise of control*. New York, NY: W. H. Freeman.

Bandura, A., & Mischel, W. (1965). Modifications of self-imposed delay of reward through exposure to live and symbolic models. *Journal of Personality and Social Psychology, 2*, 698–705. doi:10.1037/h0022655.

Bembenutty, H. (2006, April). *Preservice teachers' help-seeking tendencies and self-regulation of learning*. Paper presented at the annual meeting of the American Educational Research Association. San Francisco, CA.

Bembenutty, H. (2010). Homework completion: The role of self-efficacy, delay of gratification, and self-regulatory processes. *International Journal of Educational and Psychological Assessment, 6*(1), 1–20.

Bembenutty, H. (2013). The triumph of homework completion through a learning academy of self-regulation. In H. Bembenutty, T. J. Cleary & A. Kitsantas (Eds.), *Applications of self-regulated learning across diverse disciplines: A Tribute to Barry J. Zimmerman*. Charlotte, NC: Information Age Publishing.

Bembenutty, H., & Chen, P. P. (2005). Self-efficacy and delay of gratification. *Academic Exchange Quarterly, 9*(4), 78–86.

Bembenutty, H., & Karabenick, S. A. (1998). Academic delay of gratification. *Learning and Individual Differences, 10*, 329–346. doi:10.1016/S1041-6080(99)80126-5.

Bembenutty, H., & Karabenick, S. A. (2004). Inherent association between academic delay of gratification, future time perspective, and self-regulated learning. *Educational Psychology Review, 16*(1), 35–57. doi:10.1023/B:EDPR.0000012344.34008.5c.

Bembenutty, H., & White, M. C. (2013). Academic performance and satisfaction with homework completion among college students. *Learning and Individual Differences, 24,* 83–88. doi:10.1016/j.lindif.2012.10.013.

Bennett, C. (2002). Enhancing ethnic diversity at a big ten university through project TEAM: A case study in teacher education. *Educational Researcher, 31*(2), 21–29.

Boekaerts, M. (1997). Self-regulated learning: A new concept embraced by researchers, policy makers, educators, teachers, and students. *Learning and Instruction, 7*(2), 161–186.

Boekaerts, M., & Niemivirta, M. (2000). Self-regulated learning: Finding a balance between learning goals and ego-protective goals. In M. Boekaerts, P. R. Pintrich, & M. Zeidner (Eds.), *Handbook of self-regulation* (pp. 417–451). San Diego, CA: Academic Press.

Boyd, D., Grossman, P., Lankford, H., Loeb, S., Michelli, N., & Wyckoff, J. (2006). Complex by design: Investigating pathways into teaching in New York City schools. *Journal of Teacher Education, 57,* 155–166.

Caldwell, L. D., & Siwatu, K. O. (2003). Promoting academic persistence in African American and Latino high school students: The educational navigation skills seminar. *High School Journal, 87,* 30–38.

Carr, M., Borkowski, J. G., & Maxwell, S. E. (1991). Motivational components of underachievement. *Developmental Psychology, 27,* 108–118.

Deci, E. L. (1975). *Intrinsic motivation.* New York: Plenum.

Deci, E. L., & Ryan, R. M. (1985). *Intrinsic motivation and self-determination in human behavior.* New York: Plenum.

Dembo, M. H. (2001). Learning to teach is not enough: Future teachers also need to learn how to learn. *Teacher Education Quarterly, 28*(4), 23–35.

DiBenedetto, M. K., & White, M. C. (2013). Applying the model of development of self-regulatory competence to mentoring. In H. Bembenutty, T. J. Cleary, & A. Kitsantas (Eds.), *Applications of self-regulated learning across diverse disciplines: A tribute to Barry J. Zimmerman* (pp. 445–472). Charlotte, NC: Information Age Publishing.

Epstein, J. L. (2005). School-initiated family and community partnerships. In T. Erb (Ed.), *This we believe in action: Implementing successful middle level schools* (pp. 77–96). Westerville, OH: National Middle School Association.

Garcia, T., & Pintrich, P. R. (1996). The effects of autonomy on motivation and performance in the college classroom. *Contemporary Educational Psychology, 21*(4), 477–486. doi:10.1006/ceps.1996.0032.

Gonzalez, J. (1997). Recruiting and training minority teachers: Student views of the preservice program. *Equity and Excellence in Education, 30*(1), 56–64.

Gordon, S. (1999). *An instrument for exploring students' approaches to learning statistics.* Paper presented at the annual meeting of the American Educational Research Association (Montreal, Canada, April 1999). http://ericae.net/ericdc/ED440142.htm.

Haberman, M. (2000). Increasing the number of high-quality African American teachers in urban schools. *Journal of Instructional Psychology, 26,* 208–212.

Karabenick, S. A. (2004). Perceived achievement goal structure and college student help seeking. *Journal of Educational Psychology, 96,* 569–581.

Karabenick, S. A., & Berger, J. (2013). Help seeking as a self-regulated learning strategy. In H. Bembenutty, T. J. Cleary, & A. Kitsantas (Eds.), *Applications of self-regulated learning across diverse disciplines: A Tribute to Barry J. Zimmerman* (pp.237–261). Charlotte, NC: Information Age Publishing.

Karabenick, S. A., & Newman, R. S. (2006). *Help seeking in academic setting: Goals, groups, and contexts.* Mahwah, NJ: Lawrence Erlbaum Associates Publishers.

Keller, B. (2007). More minority teachers earn nation certification. *Education Week, 26*(21), 14.

Ley, K., & Young, D. (1998). Self-regulation in underprepared (developmental) and regular admission college students. *Contemporary Educational Psychology, 23,* 42–64.

McIntosh, S., & Norwood, P. (2004). The power of testing investigating minority teachers' responses to certification examination questions. *Urban Education, 39*(1), 33–51.

Mischel, W. (2014). *The marshmallow test: Mastering self-control*. New York, NY: Little, Brown and Company.

Nelson-Le Gall, S. (1981). Help-seeking: An understudied problem-solving skill in children. *Developmental Review, 1*(3), 224–246. doi:10.1016/0273-2297(81)90019-8.

Newman, R. (1998). Adaptive help-seeking: A role of social interaction n self-regulated learning. In S. A. Karabenick (Ed.), *Strategic help seeking. Implications for learning and teaching* (pp. 13–37). Mahweh, NJ: Lawrence Erlbaum Associates.

Pajares, F. (1996). Self-efficacy beliefs in achievement settings. *Review of Educational Research, 66*, 543–578. doi:10.3102/00346543066004543.

Paris, S. G., & Paris, A. H. (2001). Classroom applications of research on self-regulated learning. *Educational Psychologist, 36*(2), 89–101.

Pintrich, P. R. (1999). The role of motivation in promoting and sustaining self-regulated learning. *International Journal of Educational Research, 31*(6), 459–470.

Pintrich, P. R., & De Groot, E. V. (1990). Motivational and self-regulated learning components of classroom academic performance. *Journal of Educational Psychology, 82*(1), 33–40.

Pintrich, P. R., Smith, D. A. F., Garcia, T., & McKeachie, W. J. (1993). Reliability and predictive validity of the motivated strategies for learning questionnaire (MSLQ). *Educational and Psychological Measurement, 53*, 801–813.

Randi, J. (2004). Teachers as self-regulated learners. *Teachers College Record, 106*(9), 1825–1853.

Randi, J., Corno, L., & Johnson, E. (2011). Transitioning from college classroom to teaching career: Self-regulation in prospective teachers. *New Directions for Teaching and Learning, 2011*(126), 89–98.

Robbins, S. B., Lauver, K., Le, H., Davis, D., Langley, R., & Carlstrom, A. (2004). Do psychological and study skill factors predict college outcomes? A meta-analysis. *Psychological Bulletin, 130*(2), 261–288.

Schmitz, B., Klug, J., & Schmidt, M. (2011). Assessing self-regulated learning using diary measures with university students. In *Handbook of self-regulation of learning and performance* (pp. 251–265).

Schmitz, B., & Wiese, B. S. (2006). New perspectives for the evaluation of training sessions in self-regulated learning: Time-series analyses of diary data. *Contemporary Educational Psychology, 31*(1), 64–96.

Schunk, D. H. (2001). Social cognitive theory and self-regulated learning. In B. J. Zimmerman & D. H. Schunk (Eds.), *Self-regulated learning and academic achievement. Theoretical perspectives* (pp. 125–152). Mahwah, NJ: Lawrence Erlbaum Associates.

Schunk, D. H. (2003). Self-efficacy for reading and writing: Influence of modeling, goal setting, and self-evaluation. *Reading and Writing Quarterly, 19*, 159–172. doi:10.1080/10573560308219.

Schunk, D. H., & Pajares, F. (2009). Self-efficacy theory. In K. R. Wentzel & A. Wigfield (Eds.), *Handbook of motivation in schools* (pp. 35–53). New York, NY: Routledge.

Schunk, D. H., & Zimmerman, B. J. (1997). Social origins of self-regulatory competence. *Educational Psychologist, 3*(4), 195–208. doi:10.1207/s15326985ep3204_1.

Schunk, D. H., & Zimmerman, B. J. (2007). Influencing children's self-efficacy and self-regulation of reading and writing through modeling. *Reading and Writing Quarterly, 23*(1), 7–25. doi:10.1080/10573560600837578.

Tschannen-Moran, M., & Hoy, A. W. (2001). Teacher efficacy: Capturing an elusive construct. *Teaching and Teacher Education, 17*(7), 783–805.

Usher, E. L., & Pajares, F. (2008). Sources of self-efficacy in school: Critical review of the literature and future directions. *Review of Educational Research, 78*, 751–796. doi:10.3102/0034654308321456.

Volet, S., & Karabenick, S. A. (2006). Help Seeking in Cultural Context. In S. A. Karabenick & R. S. Newman (Eds.), *Help seeking in academic setting: Goals, groups, and contexts* (pp. 117–150). Mahwah, NJ, US: Lawrence Erlbaum Associates Publishers.

Weinstein, C. E., & Acee, T. W. (2013). Helping college students become more strategic and self-regulated learners. In H. Bembenutty, T. J. Cleary, A. Kitsantas (Eds.), *Applications of self-regulated learning across diverse disciplines: A tribute to Barry J. Zimmerman* (pp. 197–236). Charlotte, NC: Information Age Publishing.

White, M. C. (2010). Predicting success in teacher certification testing: The role of academic help-seeking. *Dissertation Abstracts International Section A, 70,* 4183.

White, M. C. (2011a). Predicting success in teacher certification testing: The role of academic Help seeking. *International Journal of Educational and Psychological Assessment, 7*(1), 24–44.

White, M. C. (2011b, April). Barry J. Zimmerman: An expert mentor through cyclical phases of self-regulatory feedback. *Online Submission.* Presented at the annual meeting of the American Educational Research Association, New Orleans.

White, M. C., & Bembenutty, H. (2013). Not all avoidance help seekers are created equal individual differences in adaptive and executive help seeking. *SAGE Open, 3*(2), 1–14. doi:10.1177/2158244013484916.

White, M. C., & DiBenedetto, M. K. (2015). *Self-regulation and the common core: Application to ELA standards.* New York, NY: Routledge.

Zimmerman, B. J. (1990). Self-regulated learning and academic achievement: An overview. *Educational Psychologist, 25*(1), 3–17.

Zimmerman, B. J. (1998). Developing self-fulfilling cycles of academic regulation: An analysis of exemplary instructional models. In D. H. Schunk & B. J. Zimmerman (Eds.), *Self-regulated learning: From teaching to self-reflective practice* (pp. 1–19). New York, NY: Guilford Press.

Zimmerman, B. J. (2004). Sociocultural influence and students' development of academic self-regulation: A social-cognitive perspective. In D. M. McInerney & S. van Etten (Eds.), *Big theories revisited: Research on sociocultural influences on motivation and learning* (pp. 139–164). Greenwich, CT: Information Age Publishing.

Zimmerman, B. J. (2013). From cognitive modeling to self-regulation: A social cognitive career path. *Educational Psychologist, 48,* 1–13. doi:10.1080/00461520.

Zimmerman, B. J., Bonner, S., & Kovach, R. (1996). *Developing self-regulated learners: Beyond achievement to self-efficacy.* Washington, DC: American Psychological Association. doi:10.1037/10213-000.

Zimmerman, B. J., Greenberg, D., & Weinstein, C. E. (1994). Self-regulating academic study time: A strategy approach. In D. H. Schunk & B. J. Zimmerman (Eds.), *Self-regulation of learning and performance* (pp. 181–202). NJ: Erlbaum.

Appendix A
Observation of Student Teaching (Maria by Instructor 1)

Part A

Teacher Candidate: __Maria_____ Observer: Instructor 1

Date: ___April 13, 2011_____ Subject: __Social Studies__

Grade Level: 4th & 5th Grades

Time (Begin) 1:10 pm_____ Time (End): 2:00 pm

Directions: Each observer will have a copy of the protocols to guide the observation of help seeking of a teacher candidate who is a student teacher in a professional classroom setting. Key actions and phrases are provided to identify adaptive help seeking, non-adaptive help seeking, help-avoidance, and perceived benefits of help seeking. The observation will consist of three phases: Data for phase one will be collected 10 min before the classroom observation; Data for phase two will be collected during the classroom observation; and data for phase three will be collected in the 10 min following the classroom observation, during the debriefing.

Criteria for questions posed by teacher candidate before and after the observed lesson (Phases 1 through 3).

1. Phrased in the form of a question.
2. Question is relevant to lesson planning and presentation.
3. Question requests an explanation of the process (adaptive) not an answer (nonadaptive).
4. The answer sought is substantive or curricular in nature? (Key Words: hint, demonstrate, and explain).
5. The problem is solved independently by the student teacher using the information provided by the supervisor/cooperating teacher/other.
6. Is there any evidence of help avoidance?
7. Is there any evidence of perceived benefits of help seeking?

© The Author(s) 2015
H. Bembenutty et al., *Developing Self-regulation of Learning and Teaching Skills Among Teacher Candidates*, SpringerBriefs in Education,
DOI 10.1007/978-94-017-9950-8

8. Is there any evidence of self-efficacy pertaining to the lesson? High or low?

A: Phase 1: Does the student ask any questions regarding the lesson about to be presented in class? What are they? Write each question below verbatim.

Observed question	Relevant (Y/N)	Adaptive (Y/N)	Applicable (Y/N)	Solution (Y/N)	HA (Y/N)	Ben (Y/N)	SE (Y/N)
1	2	3	4	5	6	7	8
(Write question here)	N	N	N	N	N	N	N

A: Phase 2: Observation of Help Seeking During Lesson Presentation
     Directions: Observers will collect data using the following criteria.

1. The observation of help seeking during the presentation of the lesson plan will begin at the moment the student teacher makes a statement which reflects the intention to begin a lesson. The observer will target help seeking during instruction as well as guided practice and differentiated instruction.

2. Observers will be targeting the following behaviors as observed in the student teacher when used as a classroom activity.

    a. Adaptive Help Seeking
    b. Non-Adaptive Help Seeking
    c. Help Avoidance
    d. Perceived Benefits of Help Seeking

3. The observer will note any overt behavior of the student teacher, which can be attributed to specific help-seeking goals using the following questions and chart of conditions and self-regulatory strategies.

Evidence of help-seeking behavior during lesson presentation	Y	N
Adaptive		
• ST is aware of his/her difficulty with lesson presentation. (Example)		N
• ST considers available resources before asking for help. (Example)		N
• ST perseveres with lesson presentation while making use of outlines, notes, hand-outs to guide instruction when he/she is struggles with content. (Example)		N
• ST uses the appropriate source of help during the LP. (Example)	Y	
• ST request for help fits the circumstances and learning environment. (Example) *Asked about a new student*	Y	
• ST processes and makes use of the help received. (Example)	Y	
Non adaptive/help avoidance		
• ST is unaware that he/she is experiencing difficulty during the LP. (Example) *Aware of time wasted on group work*	Y	
• ST struggles to present LP from memory. (Example)		N
• ST chooses to give up rather than ask for help. (Example)		N
• ST struggles to maintain focus on LP while class becomes disruptive. (Example)		N

Evidence of help-seeking behavior during lesson presentation	Y	N
Help avoidance		
• ST persists in dealing with his/her situation independently, not using resources available to manage classroom. (Example)		N
• ST does not formulate a question to invite assistance from appropriate resource. (Example)		N
Benefits of help seeking		
• Student moves ahead with LP after using resources (input from notes, cooperating teacher, reflection). (Example)	Y	

A: Phase 3: When student is debriefed (following lesson presentation), does the student ask any questions regarding the lesson presented in class? What are they? Write each question below verbatim.

Posed question (after lesson)	Relevant (Y/N)	Adaptive (Y/N)	Applicable (Y/N)	Solution (Y/N)	HA (Y/N)	Ben (Y/N)
(Write question here)	N	N	N	N	N	N

Observer reflection	Y	N
Did the student teacher experience any critical problems during the lesson? *Stated she did not ask for help*	Y	
After the LP, did the student ask for help regarding the problem?	Y	
Was the problem resolved? What approach or strategy would he/she use the next time?	Y	
What would the student do differently (reflection)?	Y	

Part B

CLASSROOM CONDITIONS: Does student teacher encourage help seeking in pupils by providing (or not providing) the following conditions?

Conditions	Y	N
Lesson teacher centered		N
Cooperative learning	Y	
Collaborative learning with teacher		N
Reciprocal questioning		N
Scaffolding		N
Co-construction of knowledge		N
Connection between help seeking and success (benefits) • Confirm work well done when adaptive help has been sought		N
Connection between help seeking and failure (avoidance) • Confirm work could have improved with adaptive help seeking		N
Facilitate teacher-student communication		N

Conditions	Y	N
Assist children with questioning skills	Y	
Respect between teacher and student	Y	
Evidence helpfulness (trust)		N
Lesson goals encourage students to ask for assistance when necessary		N
Classroom structure encourages interaction by using different structures (individual, small group, whole-class)	Y	
Encourage sense of individual control	Y	
Encourages discourse		N

Part C

Self-regulation: Student Teaching

Evidence of dimensions of academic self-regulation	Y	N
WHY: What does the student teacher do to demonstrate he/she sets goals using his/her understanding of self-efficacy? Examples of the students' motivation to self-regulate—make choice to prepare for lesson presentation		N
HOW: (1) What does the student teacher do to demonstrate how he/she chooses a task strategy? Examples of how the student teacher prepares, strategy use for memorization, preparing an outline		N
(2) Does he/she use careful planning and task analysis strategies?		
(3) What specific strategies does the student teacher use? *Used index cards with questions*		
WHEN: What does the student teacher do to set aside time to prepare lesson presentation? Example of how the student teacher uses time planning and management, self-beliefs		N
WHAT: What does the student teacher do as evidence that he/she self-monitors his/her performance, which leads to change? Examples of overt behavioral performance, note taking on reading, key terms, adjust to changing conditions and awareness of how classmates are coping with the same assignment		N
WHERE: What does the student teacher do to structure his/her environment for the best possible outcome of time allotted for lesson preparation? Example of how the student teacher regulates the physical environment where he/she can study *Worked for game on board; used cards*	Y	
WITH WHOM: What does the student teacher to seek help from appropriate resources? (selective help seeking). Example of adaptive help seeking with study partners, coaches, instructors that can help their learning (or not) *Asked for help with bell and reviewed rules for game*	Y	

Appendix B
Observation of Student Teaching
(of Maria by Instructor 2)

Part A

Teacher Candidate: __Maria_____ Observer: Teacher 2

Date: ___April 13, 2011_____ Subject: __Social Studies__

Grade Level: 4th & 5th Grades

Time (Begin) 1:10 pm_____ Time (End): 2:00 pm

Directions: Each observer will have a copy of the protocols to guide the observation of help seeking of a teacher candidate who is a student teacher in a professional classroom setting. Key actions and phrases are provided to identify adaptive help seeking, non-adaptive help seeking, help-avoidance, and perceived benefits of help seeking. The observation will consist of three phases: Data for phase one will be collected 10 min before the classroom observation; Data for phase two will be collected during the classroom observation; and data for phase three will be collected in the 10 min following the classroom observation, during the debriefing.

Criteria for questions posed by teacher candidate before and after the observed lesson (Phases 1 through 3).

9. Phrased in the form of a question.
10. Question is relevant to lesson planning and presentation.
11. Question requests an explanation of the process (adaptive) not an answer (nonadaptive).
12. The answer sought is substantitive or curricular in nature? (Key Words: hint, demonstrate, and explain).
13. The problem is solved independently by the student teacher using the information provided by the supervisor/cooperating teacher/other.
14. Is there any evidence of help avoidance?
15. Is there any evidence of perceived benefits of help seeking?
16. Is there any evidence of self-efficacy pertaining to the lesson? High or low?

© The Author(s) 2015
H. Bembenutty et al., *Developing Self-regulation of Learning and Teaching Skills Among Teacher Candidates*, SpringerBriefs in Education,
DOI 10.1007/978-94-017-9950-8

A: Phase 1: Does the student ask any questions regarding the lesson about to be presented in class? What are they? Write each question below verbatim.

Observed question	Relevant (Y/N)	Adaptive (Y/N)	Applicable (Y/N)	Solution (Y/N)	HA (Y/N)	Ben (Y/N)	SE (Y/N)
1	2	3	4	5	6	7	8
(Write question here)	N	N	N	N	N	N	N

A: Phase 2: Observation of Help Seeking During Lesson Presentation
   Directions: Observers will collect data using the following criteria.

4. The observation of help seeking during the presentation of the lesson plan will begin at the moment the student teacher makes a statement which reflects the intention to begin a lesson. The observer will target help seeking during instruction as well as guided practice and differentiated instruction.

5. Observers will be targeting the following behaviors as observed in the student teacher when used as a classroom activity.

   a.   Adaptive Help Seeking
   b.   Non-Adaptive Help Seeking
   c.   Help Avoidance
   d.   Perceived Benefits of Help Seeking

6. The observer will note any overt behavior of the student teacher, which can be attributed to specific help-seeking goals using the following questions and chart of conditions and self-regulatory strategies.

Evidence of help-seeking behavior during lesson presentation	Y	N
Adaptive		
• ST is aware of his/her difficulty with lesson presentation. (Example) *Missed name and asked the teacher*	Y	
• ST considers available resources before asking for help. (Example)	Y	
• ST perseveres with lesson presentation while making use of outlines, notes, hand-outs to guide instruction when he/she is struggles with content. (Example)		N
• ST uses the appropriate source of help during the LP. (Example) *Used note cards*	Y	
• ST request for help fits the circumstances and learning environment. (Example) *Asked teacher for help with name card and asked teacher to help hear bell*	Y	
• ST processes and makes use of the help received. (Example)	Y	
Non adaptive/help avoidance		
• ST is unaware that he/she is experiencing difficulty during the LP. (Example) *Wasting time picking teams and indicated that she should have returned to order*	Y	
• ST struggles to present LP from memory. (Example)		N
• ST chooses to give up rather than ask for help. (Example)		N
• ST struggles to maintain focus on LP while class becomes disruptive. (Example)		N

	Y	N
Evidence of help-seeking behavior during lesson presentation		
Help avoidance		
• ST persists in dealing with his/her situation independently, not using resources available to manage classroom. (Example)		N
• ST does not formulate a question to invite assistance from appropriate resource. (Example)		N
Benefits of help seeking		
• Student moves ahead with LP after using resources (input from notes, cooperating teacher, reflection). (Example)		N

A: Phase 3: When student is debriefed (following lesson presentation), does the student ask any questions regarding the lesson presented in class? What are they? Write each question below verbatim.

Posed question (after lesson)	Relevant (Y/N)	Adaptive (Y/N)	Applicable (Y/N)	Solution (Y/N)	HA (Y/N)	Ben (Y/N)
(Write question here)	N	N	N	N	N	N

	Y	N
Observer reflection		
Did the student teacher experience any critical problems during the lesson? *Stated she did not ask for help.*	Y	
After the LP, did the student ask for help regarding the problem?	Y	
Was the problem resolved? What approach or strategy would he/she use the next time?	Y	
What would the student do differently (reflection)?	Y	

Part B

CLASSROOM CONDITIONS: Does student teacher encourage help seeking in students by providing (or not providing) the following conditions?

Conditions	Y	N
Lesson teacher centered		N
Cooperative learning *Played a game*	Y	
Collaborative learning with teacher *Played a game*	Y	
Reciprocal questioning		N
Scaffolding *Used instruments*	Y	
Co-construction of knowledge	Y	
Connection between help seeking and success (benefits) • Confirm work well done when adaptive help has been sought	Y	

Conditions	Y	N
Connection between help seeking and failure (avoidance) • Confirm work could have improved with adaptive help seeking		N
Facilitate teacher-student communication		N
Assist children with questioning skills		N
Respect between teacher and student	Y	
Evidence helpfulness (trust)		N
Lesson goals encourage students to ask for assistance when necessary		N
Classroom structure encourages interaction by using different structures (individual, small group, whole-class) *Played a game and create groups*	Y	
Encourage sense of individual control	Y	
Encourages discourse	Y	

Part C

Self-regulation: Student Teaching

Evidence of dimensions of academic self-regulation	Y	N
WHY: What does the student teacher do to demonstrate he/she sets goals using his/her understanding of self-efficacy? Examples of the students' motivation to self-regulate—make choice to prepare for lesson presentation		N
HOW: (1) What does the student teacher do to demonstrate how he/she chooses a task strategy? Examples of how the student teacher prepares, strategy use for memorization, preparing an outline	Y	
(2) Does he/she use careful planning and task analysis strategies?		
(3) What specific strategies does the student teacher use? *Used index cards with questions, room design, and content*		
WHEN: What does the student teacher do to set aside time to prepare lesson presentation? Example of how the student teacher uses time planning and management, self-beliefs		N
WHAT: What does the student teacher do as evidence that he/she self-monitors his/her performance, which leads to change? Examples of overt behavioral performance, note taking on reading, key terms, adjust to changing conditions and awareness of how classmates are coping with the same assignment *Maintained classroom management, used note cards, and managed groups*	Y	
WHERE: What does the student teacher do to structure his/her environment for the best possible outcome of time allotted for lesson preparation? Example of how the student teacher regulates the physical environment where he/she can study *Room seating was great for game*	Y	
WITH WHOM: What does the student teacher do to seek help from appropriate resources? (selective help seeking). Example of adaptive help seeking with study partners, coaches, instructors that can help their learning (or not). *From cooperative teacher input*	Y	

Appendix C
Observation of Student Teaching
(Chris by Instructor 1)

Part A

Teacher Candidate: __Chris_____ Observer: _Teacher 1_

Date: ___April 6, 2011_____ Subject: _Reading_

Grade Level: 4th Grade

Time (Begin) 10:00 am_____ Time (End): 10:45 am

Directions: Each observer will have a copy of the protocols to guide the observation of help seeking of a teacher candidate who is a student teacher in a professional classroom setting. Key actions and phrases are provided to identify adaptive help seeking, non-adaptive help seeking, help-avoidance, and perceived benefits of help seeking. The observation will consist of three phases: Data for phase one will be collected 10 min before the classroom observation; Data for phase two will be collected during the classroom observation; and data for phase three will be collected in the 10 min following the classroom observation, during the debriefing.

Criteria for questions posed by teacher candidate before and after the observed lesson (Phases 1 through 3).

17. Phrased in the form of a question.
18. Question is relevant to lesson planning and presentation.
19. Question requests an explanation of the process (adaptive) not an answer (nonadaptive).
20. The answer sought is substantitive or curricular in nature? (Key Words: hint, demonstrate, and explain).
21. The problem is solved independently by the student teacher using the information provided by the supervisor/cooperating teacher/other.
22. Is there any evidence of help avoidance?

© The Author(s) 2015
H. Bembenutty et al., *Developing Self-regulation of Learning and Teaching Skills Among Teacher Candidates*, SpringerBriefs in Education,
DOI 10.1007/978-94-017-9950-8

23. Is there any evidence of perceived benefits of help seeking?
24. Is there any evidence of self-efficacy pertaining to the lesson? High or low?

A: Phase 1: Does the student ask any questions regarding the lesson about to be presented in class? What are they? Write each question below verbatim.

Observed question	Relevant (Y/N)	Adaptive (Y/N)	Applicable (Y/N)	Solution (Y/N)	HA (Y/N)	Ben (Y/N)	SE (Y/N)
1	2	3	4	5	6	7	8
(Write question here)	N	N	N	N	N	N	N

A: Phase 2: Observation of Help-Seeking During Lesson Presentation
  Directions: Observers will collect data using the following criteria.

7. The observation of help seeking during the presentation of the lesson plan will begin at the moment the student teacher makes a statement which reflects the intention to begin a lesson. The observer will target help seeking during instruction as well as guided practice and differentiated instruction.

8. Observers will be targeting the following behaviors as observed in the student teacher when used as a classroom activity.

   a. Adaptive Help Seeking
   b. Non-Adaptive Help Seeking
   c. Help Avoidance
   d. Perceived Benefits of Help Seeking

9. The observer will note any overt behavior of the student teacher, which can be attributed to specific help-seeking goals using the following questions and chart of conditions and self-regulatory strategies.

Evidence of help-seeking behavior during lesson presentation	Y	N
Adaptive		
• ST is aware of his/her difficulty with lesson presentation. (Example) *Chris asked about the flow of the lesson with new set up*	Y	
• ST considers available resources before asking for help. (Example) *Chris read TE before addressing the teacher*	Y	
• ST perseveres with lesson presentation while making use of outlines, notes, hand-outs to guide instruction when he/she is struggles with content. (Example)	Y	
• ST uses the appropriate source of help during the LP. (Example)	Y	
• ST request for help fits the circumstances and learning environment. (Example)	Y	
• ST processes and makes use of the help received. (Example)	Y	
Non adaptive/help avoidance		
• ST is unaware that he/she is experiencing difficulty during the LP. (Example)		N
• ST struggles to present LP from memory. (Example)		N

Evidence of help-seeking behavior during lesson presentation	Y	N
• ST chooses to give up rather than ask for help. (Example)		N
• ST struggles to maintain focus on LP while class becomes disruptive. (Example)		N
Help avoidance		
• ST persists in dealing with his/her situation independently, not using resources available to manage classroom. (Example)		N
• ST does not formulate a question to invite assistance from appropriate resource. (Example)		N
Benefits of help seeking		
• Student moves ahead with LP after using resources (input from notes, cooperating teacher, reflection). (Example)	Y	

A: Phase 3: When student is debriefed (following lesson presentation), does the student ask any questions regarding the lesson presented in class? What are they? Write each question below verbatim.

Posed question (after lesson)	Relevant (Y/N)	Adaptive (Y/N)	Applicable (Y/N)	Solution (Y/N)	HA (Y/N)	Ben (Y/N)
(Write question here)	N	N	N	N	N	N

Observer reflection	Y	N
Did the student teacher experience any critical problems during the lesson?		N
After the LP, did the student ask for help regarding the problem?		N
Was the problem resolved? What approach or strategy would he/she use the next time?		N
What would the student do differently (reflection)?		N

Part B

CLASSROOM CONDITIONS: Does student teacher encourage help seeking in students by providing (or not providing) the following conditions?

Conditions	Y	N
Lesson teacher centered		N
Cooperative learning	Y	
Collaborative learning with teacher	Y	
Reciprocal questioning		N
Scaffolding	Y	
Co-construction of knowledge	Y	
Connection between help seeking and success (benefits) • Confirm work well done when adaptive help has been sought		N

Conditions	Y	N
Connection between help seeking and failure (avoidance) • Confirm work could have improved with adaptive help seeking		N
Facilitate teacher-student communication	Y	
Assist children with questioning skills	Y	
Respect between teacher and student	Y	
Evidence helpfulness (trust)	Y	
Lesson goals encourage students to ask for assistance when necessary	Y	
Classroom structure encourages interaction by using different structures (individual, small group, whole-class)	Y	
Encourage sense of individual control	Y	
Encourages discourse	Y	

Part C

Self-regulation: Student Teaching

Evidence of dimensions of academic self-regulation	Y	N
WHY: What does the student teacher do to demonstrate he/she sets goals using his/her understanding of self-efficacy? Examples of the students' motivation to self-regulate—make choice to prepare for lesson presentation	Y	
HOW: (1) What does the student teacher do to demonstrate how he/she chooses a task strategy? Examples of how the student teacher prepares, strategy use for memorization, preparing an outline	Y	
(2) Does he/she use careful planning and task analysis strategies?		
(3) What specific strategies does the student teacher use?		
WHEN: What does the student teacher do to set aside time to prepare lesson presentation? Example of how the student teacher uses time planning and management, self-beliefs	Y	
WHAT: What does the student teacher do as evidence that he/she self-monitors his/her performance, which leads to change? Examples of overt behavioral performance, note taking on reading, key terms, adjust to changing conditions and awareness of how classmates are coping with the same assignment	Y	
WHERE: What does the student teacher do to structure his/her environment for the best possible outcome of time allotted for lesson preparation? Example of how the student teacher regulates the physical environment where he/she can study	Y	
WITH WHOM: What does the student teacher to seek help from appropriate resources? (selective help seeking). Example of adaptive help seeking with study partners, coaches, instructors that can help their learning (or not)	Y	

Appendix D
Direct Observation of Student Teaching (Chris by Instructor 2)

Part A

Teacher Candidate: ___Chris_____ Observer: Teacher 2

Date: ___April 6, 2011_____ Subject: _Reading____

Grade Level: 4th Grade

Time (Begin) 10:00 am_____ Time (End): 10:45 am

Directions: Each observer will have a copy of the protocols to guide the observation of help seeking of a teacher candidate who is a student teacher in a professional classroom setting. Key actions and phrases are provided to identify adaptive help seeking, non-adaptive help seeking, help-avoidance, and perceived benefits of help seeking. The observation will consist of three phases: Data for phase one will be collected 10 min before the classroom observation; Data for phase two will be collected during the classroom observation; and data for phase three will be collected in the 10 min following the classroom observation, during the debriefing.

Criteria for questions posed by teacher candidate before and after the observed lesson (Phases 1 through 3).

25. Phrased in the form of a question.
26. Question is relevant to lesson planning and presentation.
27. Question requests an explanation of the process (adaptive) not an answer (nonadaptive).
28. The answer sought is substantitive or curricular in nature? (Key Words: hint, demonstrate, and explain).
29. The problem is solved independently by the student teacher using the information provided by the supervisor/cooperating teacher/other.
30. Is there any evidence of help avoidance?

© The Author(s) 2015
H. Bembenutty et al., *Developing Self-regulation of Learning and Teaching Skills Among Teacher Candidates*, SpringerBriefs in Education,
DOI 10.1007/978-94-017-9950-8

31. Is there any evidence of perceived benefits of help seeking?
32. Is there any evidence of self-efficacy pertaining to the lesson? High or low?

A: Phase 1: Does the student ask any questions regarding the lesson about to be presented in class? What are they? Write each question below verbatim.

Observed question	Relevant (Y/N)	Adaptive (Y/N)	Applicable (Y/N)	Solution (Y/N)	HA (Y/N)	Ben (Y/N)	SE (Y/N)
1	2	3	4	5	6	7	8
(Write question here)	N	N	N	N	N	N	N

A: Phase 2: Observation of Help Seeking During Lesson Presentation
Directions: Observers will collect data using the following criteria.

10. The observation of help-seeking during the presentation of the lesson plan will begin at the moment the student teacher makes a statement which reflects the intention to begin a lesson. The observer will target help seeking during instruction as well as guided practice and differentiated instruction.

11. Observers will be targeting the following behaviors as observed in the student teacher when used as a classroom activity.

    a. Adaptive Help Seeking
    b. Non-Adaptive Help Seeking
    c. Help Avoidance
    d. Perceived Benefits of Help Seeking

12. The observer will note any overt behavior of the student teacher, which can be attributed to specific help-seeking goals using the following questions and chart of conditions and self-regulatory strategies.

Evidence of help-seeking behavior during lesson presentation	Y	N
Adaptive		
• ST is aware of his/her difficulty with lesson presentation. (Example)	Y	
• ST considers available resources before asking for help. (Example)	Y	
• ST perseveres with lesson presentation while making use of outlines, notes, hand-outs to guide instruction when he/she is struggles with content. (Example)	Y	
• ST uses the appropriate source of help during the LP. (Example)	Y	
• ST request for help fits the circumstances and learning environment. (Example)	Y	
• ST processes and makes use of the help received. (Example) *Teacher and Student Teacher consult for next step*	Y	
Non adaptive/help avoidance		
• ST is unaware that he/she is experiencing difficulty during the LP. (Example)		N
• ST struggles to present LP from memory. (Example)		N

	Y	N
Evidence of help-seeking behavior during lesson presentation	Y	N
• ST chooses to give up rather than ask for help. (Example)		N
• ST struggles to maintain focus on LP while class becomes disruptive. (Example)		N
Help avoidance		
• ST persists in dealing with his/her situation independently, not using resources available to manage classroom. (Example)		N
• ST does not formulate a question to invite assistance from appropriate resource. (Example)		N
Benefits of help seeking		
• Student moves ahead with LP after using resources (input from notes, cooperating teacher, reflection). (Example)	Y	

A: Phase 3: When student is debriefed (following lesson presentation), does the student ask any questions regarding the lesson presented in class? What are they? Write each question below verbatim.

Posed question (after lesson)	Relevant (Y/N)	Adaptive (Y/N)	Applicable (Y/N)	Solution (Y/N)	HA (Y/N)	Ben (Y/N)
(Write question here)	N	N	N	N	N	N

Observer reflection	Y	N
Did the student teacher experience any critical problems during the lesson?		N
After the LP, did the student ask for help regarding the problem?		N
Was the problem resolved? What approach or strategy would he/she use the next time?		N
What would the student do differently (reflection)?		N

Part B

CLASSROOM CONDITIONS: Does student teacher encourage help seeking in pupils by providing (or not providing) the following conditions?

Conditions	Y	N
Lesson teacher centered		N
Cooperative learning	Y	
Collaborative learning with teacher	Y	
Reciprocal questioning	Y	
Scaffolding	Y	
Co-construction of knowledge	Y	
Connection between help-seeking and success (benefits) • Confirm work well done when adaptive help has been sought	Y	
Connection between help-seeking and failure (avoidance) • Confirm work could have improved with adaptive help seeking		N

Conditions	Y	N
Facilitate teacher-student communication	Y	
Assist children with questioning skills	Y	
Respect between teacher and student	Y	
Evidence helpfulness (trust)	Y	
Lesson goals encourage students to ask for assistance when necessary	Y	
Classroom structure encourages interaction by using different structures (individual, small group, whole-class)	Y	
Encourage sense of individual control	Y	
Encourages discourse	Y	

Part C

Self-regulation: Student Teaching

Evidence of dimensions of academic self-regulation	Y	N
WHY: What does the student teacher do to demonstrate he/she sets goals using his/her understanding of self-efficacy? Examples of the students' motivation to self-regulate—make choice to prepare for lesson presentation	Y	
HOW: (1) What does the student teacher do to demonstrate how he/she chooses a task strategy? Examples of how the student teacher prepares, strategy use for memorization, preparing an outline	Y	
(2) Does he/she use careful planning and task analysis strategies?		
(3) What specific strategies does the student teacher use?		
WHEN: What does the student teacher do to set aside time to prepare lesson presentation? Example of how the student teacher uses time planning and management, self-beliefs	Y	
WHAT: What does the student teacher do as evidence that he/she self-monitors his/her performance, which leads to change? Examples of overt behavioral performance, note taking on reading, key terms, adjust to changing conditions and awareness of how classmates are coping with the same assignment	Y	
WHERE: What does the student teacher do to structure his/her environment for the best possible outcome of time allotted for lesson preparation? Example of how the student teacher regulates the physical environment where he/she can study	Y	
WITH WHOM: What does the student teacher to seek help from appropriate resources? (selective help seeking). Example of adaptive help seeking with study partners, coaches, instructors that can help their learning (or not)	Y	

Appendix E
Student Teaching in Person Interview
(Chris by Instructor 2)

Teacher Candidate: __Chris__   Date: __April 18, 2010__   Interviewer: Instructor 2

Directions: The interviewers will have a copy of the guiding questions. They will take turns to ask questions. If the student's response is not sufficient or clear, the interviewer could prompt the student to provide more information or will have a follow up question. Interviewers should take notes and write verbatim any important answers by the student.

1. How do you perceive your students? FOLLOW UP QUESTIONS: (e.g., Can all of the students learn? What are the students' responsibilities in the classroom? What are your responsibilities on their learning?)

1	2	3	4	5	6	7
Negative perception						Highly positive perception

Note: When I have had disruptive students, I have been able to intervene one to one and follow up with informal talks. I often look at a student's body language first to see if there is a behavior problem about to occur. That is when I sit with the student to prevent an outburst, and I intervene before anything happens. This is how I build relationships with disruptive students, and I see it as one of my most important roles in the classroom. When I am teaching, I use post it notes to remind students of their strengths. Phrases such as: "You are smart!" "You have strengths!" "You are learning!" always build confidence.

I absolutely believe that all children can learn! It is not one size fits all. I teach in sequential steps so that every student is able to move forward a

© The Author(s) 2015
H. Bembenutty et al., *Developing Self-regulation of Learning and Teaching Skills Among Teacher Candidates*, SpringerBriefs in Education,
DOI 10.1007/978-94-017-9950-8

little bit at a time. My responsibility includes that the objectives set by the curriculum and the standards for learning are met. I self-monitor how well I am meeting my objectives and I reflect on how well I have met my goals at the end of each lesson. I own what happens in the classroom; I am primarily responsible for the learning that takes place!

2. How confident are you that you can teach your students? FOLLOW UP QUESTIONS: (e.g., Can you motivate all learners? Do you have all the necessary skills to help all your students? What is your role on your students' learning experience? How much does their learning and academic achievements depend on you?)

       1   2   3   4   5   6   7
       Very low   Very high
       confidence   confidence

Note: Highly confident. Setting goals and making progress towards those goals as a team is important. Also, what may work 1 week may not work the next, so I have to acquire skills that help me adapt to specific learning situations.

I can motivate my students through praise and deter poor behavior by emphasizing strengths. If a student has difficulty with an assignment, I can shorten the assignment rather than see him frustrated. Gifted students are especially a challenge. keeping them motivated can be done by asking them to work with other students as peer tutors. Also, students with cognitive dysfunctions can benefit from peer tutoring; however, in their case, I would work with a specialist to determine what strategies would work best. As far as helping all students learn, theories are good to know, but at times the theories don't work, and you make a decision on the spot what to do if your students are not learning. Getting help from an appropriate resource is an effective way to make sure my students achieve. At the end of the day, I do whatever I need to do for the students, even if it is not readily available and I need to find it.

3. Are you a self-regulated teacher candidate? FOLLOW UP QUESTIONS: (e.g., How? Give an example.)

       1   2   3   4   5   6   7
       Expressed low   Expressed high
       self-regulation   self-regulation

Note: I would say I am self-regulated. I manage my time well. I prepare and rehearse my lessons. I am highly organized and maintain an ongoing set of post-its as reminders of what I need to do, when I need to do it, and where I need to be. I re-evaluate lessons at the end and ask myself "Did I accomplish what I set out to do? What can I change?" I use feedback to make adjustments to my lesson plans from my supervisor's comments on my lesson planning.

4. Please tell us about your efforts to seek help when a lesson plan or a class does not go well. FOLLOW UP QUESTIONS: (e.g., When the students misbehave, to get information for your lesson, when you do not understand something, when the tasks are too difficult for you to accomplish on your own, by whom, to learn or to get answers?)

| 1 | 2 | 3 | 4 | 5 | 6 | 7 |

Do not   Very often
seek help   seek help

Note: I am a help-seeker, and I am always looking for the best resources to meet my particular need. Especially when I know a lesson plan and performance could be improved. I email my cooperating teacher following a lesson and ask what I could have done better. I often have to make the decision to stop working and look for assistance if I am stuck with my lesson planning. I have had a moment when the lesson I was delivering was not going well, that is when I looked to my cooperating teacher to get on the spot assistance to move the lesson in a different direction. I had difficulty modifying lessons for differentiated instruction; the math coach was very helpful regarding how to add visuals to the same lesson for learners who needed adapted worksheets. The cooperating teacher, other student teachers, my supervisor, and the math coach have all been supportive and shared their expertise with me throughout my student teaching.

5. Can you help your students to be self-regulated learners? FOLLOW UP QUESTIONS: (e.g., How? Give an example.)

| 1 | 2 | 3 | 4 | 5 | 6 | 7 |

Very low   Very high
confidence   confidence

Note: My modeling of organizational strategies and self-regulation is the best way I can help my students become self-regulated. By creating an environment that is goal directed, setting goals for myself, and for individual students, I remain a learner. I think the model of the teacher as a learner, sometimes struggling to learn something new, is a great way to help students become self-regulated beginning in the early grades.

6. Can you help your students to delay gratification for the sake of learning? FOLLOW UP QUESTIONS: (e.g., How? Give an example.)

           1   2   3   4   5   6   7
         Very low   Very high
         confidence   confidence

Note: I can do this to a certain degree. I believe I can set up our learning environment with a system of rewards that helps the students delay gratification for the sake of learning. I have learned how to spend less time doing things that are more enjoyable to remain available after school to provide extra help for struggling students. I share my own experiences with my students and demonstrate how to attribute success or failure to time on task. I value my time more now than I had before I student taught, and I set priorities for myself. In turn, I help my students set priorities and receive rewards for delaying gratification over a set period of time.

7. What is your philosophy of teaching? FOLLOW UP QUESTIONS: (e.g., Why? Tell us about your classroom management beliefs. What are some of the classroom management strategies that you use in your classroom?)

           1   2   3   4   5   6   7
         Very unclear   Very clear
         classroom management   classroom management

Note: My philosophy of teaching begins with all children can learn but they are wired differently. They gravitate to caring individuals and want to emulate them. The teacher creates the classroom environment where the student is valued and speaks words of respect into their lives. The more the students experience this type of respect the more they believe they deserve it. My classroom management beliefs include that the teacher is an authority that can be both respected and approachable. The teacher can be both the disciplinarian and fun. My respect model is reciprocal, Teacher: Student, then the Student: Teacher. I also respect the role of the parent and consider them active members of my classroom. I am ready to conference and provide help for parents when needed.

8. Tell us about how you perceive or expect to help students from diverse backgrounds (e.g., ethnicity, gender, cognitive or physical disability, language, and exceptionality).

1	2	3	4	5	6	7
Very low understanding						Very high understanding

Note: My background is diverse. I don't stereotype, and individual diversity is respected. I have never seen ethnicity as a difference; it is a contribution to the learning environment. I can make my classroom appealing to all students. If it is history lesson, Obama is the role model, there are other historical figures who are role models that I like to include in my lessons. As far as gender, I believe in teaching values, being kind to each other, equality, and fairness. My goals for students who are exceptional learners are highly individualized so they are successful participants in the learning environment. When working with students who are ELL, I provide worksheets in their first language until they become more familiar with English so they can participate in learning activities.

9. How has the college's educational program influenced your teaching practice and your philosophy of classroom management?

1	2	3	4	5	6	7
Not helped at all						Helped a lot

Note: The college provided me with a safe atmosphere. My self-efficacy for learning increased over time during my time in many different types of classes. I have been stretched, taught to set goals, and worked hard to attain each goal. There is a family atmosphere at the college, especially in the school of education. Early on, expectations were set, I was closely monitored, and feedback was provided. Now I feel empowered to leave and become a teacher and continue my learning in a Master's program.

Appendix F
Post-graduation Online Interview

Teacher Candidate: _____Jaime_____   Date: __6/22/12_____

Are you attending a college? Yes__X___ No_____

What is the name of the college's program<u>Master of Science in Education (MS Ed)</u>_____

Are you currently teaching? Yes__X_____ No_____

Where are you teaching? <u>Religious School</u>_____

What grade level(s) and subject(s) are you teaching?___<u>Kindergarten Teacher</u>_____

Purpose: When you were an undergraduate student at the college, you shared with us your thoughts, experiences, and beliefs related to your academic and student teaching experiences. A full year has passed, and we would like to learn about your current beliefs and experiences related to your academic and professional experiences.

Below, we have included some questions to guide you while you share with us your experiences. There is no right or wrong answer. You can respond to all the questions or only to those you are comfortable answering. Your answer will not affect your job or academic status or your relationship with your current or former educators. Thus, your answers can be very honest. Part of your answers may be included anonymously in a publication (e.g., a book or article), thus, your name will not be included in any document and your answers will not be part of your official record at the college. A random code number will be assigned to your answers to replace your name on this document. Although there is not financial compensation for your participation, we will make available to you an online version of any publication containing information you share with us. If you have concerns or questions pertaining the questions or your participation in this project, please contact the directors of the program.

© The Author(s) 2015
H. Bembenutty et al., *Developing Self-regulation of Learning and Teaching Skills Among Teacher Candidates*, SpringerBriefs in Education,
DOI 10.1007/978-94-017-9950-8

Directions: After reading the questions, please circle the number between 1 and 7 that best reflects your actual beliefs and experiences. Then, answer the question by typing your answer within the space provided but you can use more space if it is needed. You can write as much and as freely as you can. Please be very specific in your answers by providing detailed examples of your experiences or by clearly explaining your beliefs.

1. How do you perceive your students? Can all of the students learn? What are the students' responsibilities in the classroom? What are your responsibilities on their learning)?

1	2	3	4	5	6	7
Negative						Highly positive
perception						perception

Response to the question(s):

I see my students as very capable and intelligent young boys and girls that have great potential. I only look at their weaknesses as an opportunity for their strengths to shine through. I believe that all of my students are able to learn. Every child is different, and I can find any possible way to help them overcome their weaknesses by being the best teacher that I can be to them. Five important things that I feel I need as a teacher are love, patience, passion, knowledge, and discipline. I need to make sure I have all the resources I need. If I am lacking in any necessities, I need to do whatever it takes to get them so that I can support the students' learning. It will be difficult to accomplish this task if I do not have any passion motivating me to do so. I need to have patience when my students are not getting the material and are getting frustrated. I also need to make sure I show them love and discipline. I had a situation with a kindergartner that demonstrates the importance of patience. One of my students was not doing well in school and I could see the frustration in his eyes. However, I did not let this frustrate me as well because the students can sense it if I did. I used many resources, became knowledgeable in what I thought I needed to know that would help, and continued working with him day by day patiently. With the help from his family and myself, he improved dramatically! In order to learn, the students' responsibilities are to be attentive, respectful, follow instructions, be obedient, be willing to learn, believe in themselves, and have fun. When students begin to take on these simple responsibilities, they will be able to succeed in school with the help of the teacher and family.

2. How confident are you that you can teach your students? Can you motivate all learners? Do you have all the necessary skills to help all your students? What is your role on your students' learning experience? How much does their learning and academic achievements depend on you?

1	2	3	4	5	6	7
Very low confidence						Very high confidence

Response to the question(s):

In the beginning of my student teaching, my confidence was very low. It was not until I began teaching in my own classroom that my confidence increased tremendously. I am very confident in knowing that I can teach my students. I can definitely motivate my learners. I believe I have all the necessary skills to help my students depending on what types of students I have and their learning differences. For example, since I am a perfectionist, I need to make sure I am knowledgeable about every aspect of cerebral palsy before I begin to teach a child that has cerebral palsy. In my current classroom I have worked hard to develop all the skills that I need to help all of my students. If I were placed in a classroom filled with students of disabilities, I would need to make sure I have all the resources I need as well as the knowledge special education methods. I believe that my role is very important when it comes to the students' learning experience. I need to make sure I consistently creating a positive and healthy learning environment within the classroom as well as maintaining a consistent routine and effective teaching style for all my students. I personally feel that my teaching will influence his or her learning and academic achievement.

3. Are you a self-regulated student (or teacher if you are teaching? How? Give examples.)?

1	2	3	4	5	6	7
Very low self-regulated						Very highly self-regulated

Response to the question(s):

I believe that I am very highly self-regulated as a teacher because I take full control of and evaluate my own learning and behavior in the classroom. I am very much aware of my learning style and make sure to monitor my teaching as well as the students' learning. My time management has improved tremendously. I would not have improved my time management if I did not continue self-monitoring and worked through trial and error, reflecting on my misuse of time and working towards adjusting my schedule. I have also improved greatly in partnering with other teachers and parents to help the student as well as my own teaching abilities.

4. Please tell us about your efforts to seek help when a lesson plan or a class do not go well (e.g., when the students misbehave, to get information for your lesson, when you do not understand something, when the tasks are too difficult for you to accomplish on your own, by whom, to learn or to get answers).

1   2   3   4   5   6   7

Do not   Very often

seek help   seek help

Response to the question(s):

I believe that my help seeking has increased tremendously since I began teaching. I realized that I had lots of questions that needed answers. Throughout my teaching experience, I have asked for help from other teachers, parents, peers, friends, and family and have received more knowledge than I did before I ever asked. It is always healthy to hear another opinion besides your own, and it has always been an advantage on my part.

5. Can you help your students to be self-regulated learners? How? Give examples.

1   2   3   4   5   6   7

Very low   Very high

confidence   confidence

Response to the question(s):

I am very confident that I can help my students become self-regulated learners. I can be sure to give them enough guidance while working on a task so that 1 day they can complete the task all by themselves. For example, when one of my students keeps asking for my help in reading certain words and sounding it out, I decided to continue guiding and teaching him until I felt he was ready to read and sound out the words on his own. Once I felt I he was gaining confidence, I left him to do the work on his own, and I didn't check his work until the very end of the lesson. He would look at me every now and again and tell me he couldn't do a problem, or it was too hard for him, but I kept telling him he could do it. Before I knew it, he was able to do it on his own without my help! I also am sure to give my students the duties of a monitor in the classroom to help them develop independence, self-regulation, and responsibility.

6. Can you help your students to delay gratification for the sake of learning? How? Give examples.

1	2	3	4	5	6	7
Very low confidence						Very high confidence

Response to the question(s):

I am well able to help my students delay gratification for the sake of learning. Although my students often show their natural tendencies to want the easy way out in learning a difficult concept, I make sure to challenge them and reward them when I see they are trying to do their best work. The children see this and they are motivated by these rewards. For future tasks I give out rewards less often so that the children can be motivated to do the work without a reward on their mind, but rather just to do well in school. For example, I give out random stickers to students who I see are improving or giving their best effort to complete a task and as a result I have seen a group of students begin to really enjoy the subject (to their surprise) without being focused on the reward. For example, one of my students who enjoys writing had to be pushed and rewarded by me when I saw fit. Eventually he would do the writing task on his own without me rewarding him. I also make sure to have playtime at the end and during the school day so that my students are not focused on playing, but on learning. Even throughout the day while the students are working, if I see they are very attentive and focused on schoolwork, I give them free time or rewards. I have trained my children to think that work comes first, then play.

7. What is your philosophy of teaching? Why? Tell us about your classroom management beliefs. What are some of the classroom management strategies that you use in your classroom?

1	2	3	4	5	6	7

Very unclear   Very highly
classroom management skills   classroom management skills

Response to the question(s):

I strongly believe that teachers can help students reach their fullest potential, or at least direct them into the right path to continue on in reaching their fullest potential. Every child is capable of learning. Creating a positive and healthy learning environment, being a teacher that replicates good character as well as good teaching strategies, and making sure the family is involved in the child's life are important for the child to be on track to succeed in school. The teacher needs to show love, patience, passion, knowledge, and discipline in the classroom. I believe that a teacher holds a big responsibility in the child's learning and the parents play an even bigger role in the child's lives. When teaching, I make sure I have a simple routine for every procedure that can easily be followed by the class. I believe that having daily routines can help students increase their independence and confidence in the classroom. I make sure to not only create a positive learning environment, but I create simple rules from the beginning of the school year that the students can follow.

I also have a classroom management chart to monitor my students' behavior each day. If the child has a green, they are well behaved. If the child has a yellow (or three strikes), they were not doing so well, and have timeout during playtime, parties, or any free time. If the child has a red (more than three strikes), they have automatically lose playtime, they will do classwork. There will possibly be a talk with the parent, depending on the severity of the situation. One thing I do not tolerate is when students hit each other, use profanity, or steal from others. When that happens, it is an automatic red at times depending on the circumstances. I also have a classroom rewards points jar which helps monitor the behavior of the whole class in general. If all of the students received green, I place a small pompom in the jar. When the children have reached 10 pompoms/points, they will be rewarded with an ice cream party. I like to monitor behavior not only individually, but also as a group so that the students feel like a team.

All of these activities encourage my student to self-monitor their own behavior. During this school year, I was faced with a situation when I had a student with behavior problems act out on a daily basis. I felt that he needed a specific intervention because his behavior interfered with his academic performance. I created a special behavior chart that I placed on his desk every day that I would sign at the end of the day, and send to the parent. The behavior chart had five pictures depicting behaviors (using your inside voice, raising your hand, listening to the teacher, finishing your work, and keeping your hands to yourself). If the child did not follow to do as one of the pictures demonstrates, he would take his pencil and mark an X next to the picture. I had him do it himself so that he could self-monitor his behavior and begin to understand what he was doing wrong. I thought this was the best way to deal with his acting out since at times he is very disorganized and out of focus when he misbehaves. How he controlled his behavior would determine whether or not he was rewarded. When this child did something positive during the day, I would then erase an X and put a check to replace it. The reason for this was to make him feel as if I am not only acknowledging his mistakes, but his good behavior as well. Thankfully, this behavior chart has really improved his behavior. I also make sure the chart is sent to the parent afterschool so that there are no gaps or miscommunications between the child, the parent, and the school. I strongly believe there needs to be a good parent-teacher-school communication to help the child's learning to improve.

8. Tell us about how you perceive or expect to help students from diverse backgrounds (e.g., ethnicity, gender, cognitive or physical disability, language, and exceptionality)?

| 1 | 2 | 3 | 4 | 5 | 6 | 7 |

Very low
Understanding of diversity

Very High
understanding of diversity

Response to the question(s):

I gladly welcome every student that enters my classroom. I make sure to learn as much as I can about each student's background so I can understand influences of whatever race, gender, religion, language, exceptionality, or disability is represented in my classroom. I also make sure to do research on their learning and physical needs, so that I can help them to the best of my ability. I want to make sure I am knowledgeable and have the proper resources that I need to take care of my students in a way that will help their learning. For example, I was very sensitive to the needs of one of my students who had a speech impediment and required occupational therapy. As time went by, I realized I needed to reduce the amount of sentences he wrote for writing tasks because he was not able to complete five sentences in the time allotted. It was not because of laziness or distraction; it was because his hands would hurt and it was too much writing for him. I would also modify the home work and sometimes classwork for him as needed. I found these accommodations to be very helpful when him can work at his pace; not mine. As time progressed, I began seeing him improve and I continued challenging him until eventually he was able to do the same amount of sentences as the entire class was doing. With that said, I am very mindful of every child and their needs and try my very best to have them fulfill their highest potential in learning, working from their level. Teaching is for them to learn, it is not about me; it is about the student.

9. How has the college's educational program influenced your teaching practice and your philosophy of classroom management? (If you are not teaching, answer the question in relation to your current education.)

1	2	3	4	5	6	7
No helped at all						Helped a lot

Response to the question(s):

The School of Education has helped me tremendously in my teaching practices, philosophy of education, and classroom management strategies. Most of my learning in teaching and classroom management really started from my student teaching. Once I began teaching in my own classroom, everything I had learned in school and in student teaching came into play. Once I was able to apply what I've learned in both, I was able to manage my classroom very well. Although I am learning something new each day, I have acquired much knowledge and feedback on my teaching through the college.

Printed in the United States
By Bookmasters